By the same author:
*Cruising Guide to Anglesey and the Menai Strait.* James Laver Ltd (1977)
*Cruising Guide to the Isle of Man.* James Laver Ltd (1978)
*A Yachtsman's Navigation.* James Laver Ltd (1978)
*The Englishman's Watch.* John Sherrat & Son Ltd (1979)
*The Fusee Lever Watch.* John Sherrat & Son Ltd (1981)
and books on medical matters.

# Irish Sea and Bristol Channel Pilot

Dr ROBERT KEMP

ADLARD COLES LIMITED
**GRANADA PUBLISHING**
London Toronto Sydney New York

Published by Granada Publishing in
Adlard Coles Limited 1983
Second edition
First published 1976

Granada Publishing Limited
Frogmore, St Albans, Herts AL2 2NF
and
36 Golden Square, London W1R 4AH
515 Madison Avenue, New York, NY 10022, USA
117 York Street, Sydney, NSW 2000, Australia
100 Skyway Avenue, Rexdale, Ontario M9W 3A6, Canada
61 Beach Road, Auckland, New Zealand

ISBN 0 229 11683 3
Printed in Great Britain by
Fletchers & Son Ltd, Norwich

Granada ®
Granada Publishing ®

## Acknowledgements

The chartlets in this book are mostly based on the appropriate Admiralty chart, with the kind permission of the Controller, HM Stationery Office and the Hydrographer of the Navy; one or two are partly based on personal observation and/or local tourist office hand-outs.

Some of the chartlets are reproduced from the first edition; those for Anglesey come from my book *Cruising Guide to Anglesey*, and were drawn for me by F G Quigley; figures 6 and 7 were drawn by John Heyworth; those for the Isle of Man come from my book *Cruising Guide to the Isle of Man*, and were drawn by Carl Salkeld; those for Southern Ireland and for the Bristol Channel were drawn by Imray, Laurie, Norie and Wilson.

The section on the South Coast of Ireland was contributed by Bob Evans, who also supplied all the accompanying photographs. The two sections on the Bristol Channel and Severn Estuary were contributed by Jeremy Howard-Williams, who also took all the accompanying photographs. The remaining photographs in the book were taken by myself.

# Contents

## List of passage and harbour plans

## List of Plates

| | | |
|---|---|---|
| 1 Rosslare | 33 Douglas | 65 Barmouth |
| 2 Arklow | 34 Castletown | 66 Barmouth |
| 3 Dalkey Island | 35 Chicken Rock | 67 Fishguard |
| 4 Dunleary | 36 Port St Mary | 68 Fishguard |
| 5 Kish Bank Tower | 37 Calf Sound | 69 Solva |
| 6 Howth Harbour | 38 Port Erin | 70 Dunmore East |
| 7 Balbriggan | 39 Peel | 71 Youghal |
| 8 Drogheda | 40 Ramsey | 72 Capel Island |
| 9 Port Oriel | 41 Ramsey | 73 East Passage |
| 10 Kilkeel | 42 Laxey | 74 Kinsale |
| 11 St John's Point | 43 Laxey | 75 Old Head of Kinsale |
| 12 Ardglass | 44 Southport | 76 Glandore |
| 13 Portavogie | 45 Great Ormes Head | 77 Baltimore Harbour |
| 14 Mew Island | 46 Conway | 78 Clear Island |
| 15 Donaghadee | 47 Conway | 79 Schull |
| 16 Bangor | 48 Puffin Island | 80 Long Island |
| 17 Larne | 49 Redwharf Bay | 81 Tenby |
| 18 West Maiden | 50 Lynas Point | 82 Saundersfoot |
| 19 East Maiden | 51 Wylfa Head | 83 Mumbles Head |
| 20 Corsewell Point | 52 The Skerries | 84 Swansea |
| 21 Portpatrick | 53 Holyhead | 85 Port Talbot |
| 22 Portpatrick | 54 Holy Island | 86a Porthcawl |
| 23 Workington | 55 Pilot's Cove | 86b Porthcawl |
| 24 Walney Island | 56 The Swellies | 87 Barry |
| 25 Barrow | 57 Beaumaris | 88 Barry Old Harbour |
| 26 Piel Island | 58 Port Penrhyn | 89 Cardiff |
| 27 Roa Island | 59 The Swellies | 90 St Ives |
| 28 Barrow Channel | 60 Caernarvon | 91 Newquay |
| 29 Fleetwood | 61 Pwllheli | 92 Padstow |
| 30 Glasson Dock | 62 Pwllheli | 93 Burnham on Sea |
| 31 Heysham | 63 Portmadoc | 94 Weston super Mare |
| 32 Douglas Head | 64 Portmadoc | 95 Avonmouth |

# Introduction

Frank Cowper was probably the first to publish a systematic round-the-coast guide for 'amateur yachtsmen', having started his sailing about a hundred years ago. His five volumes of *Sea Tours* appeared in the early 1890's, with the relative sector entitled *Land's End to the Mull of Galloway*. These and his other books are well out of print (though luckily most are in my library), but my reason for harking back to the beginning of yachting is not simply historical. It is to give one the chance to see how things have changed over the last century in face of the great increase in the number of pleasure craft. The significant finding is that on the eastern side of the Irish Sea there have been hardly any changes or improvements, so that today's yachts have to make do with what was already there in Cowper's time. In contrast, on the Irish coast many of the harbours have been rebuilt (Howth being an example), while there are plans for marinas in Dunleary, Howth, and Belfast Lough.

Thus much of the cruising to be described could be tagged as unspoilt, traditional, or downright primitive. The tidal rises are high, the streams strong, the winds fresh and the skies rather gloomy. Many of the harbours are tidal and not very secure, while moorings are often exposed. Of marinas, there is currently only one in operation in the Irish Sea – at Glasson Dock in Morecambe Bay; it is a far cry from today's idiom of cruising from one marina to the next. Thus sailing is exciting, exacting and rewarding in the old-fashioned way. Having served a long apprenticeship to these rough conditions, I am now fully converted to the need for marinas if such a magnificent cruising ground as the Irish Sea is to come into its own. However, yachting opinion in the north west moves slowly, so that owners of quite valuable boats are still content, as we shall see, to keep them on exposed moorings. While insurance companies are now beginning to penalise insecure berths, and there is plenty of marina potential in unused docks, opinion is not yet ready to accept the cost. Writing particularly for those who are exploring new ground for the first time, I have to risk offending local loyalties by mentioning the weaknesses of harbours exposed by adverse conditions. However, visitors must be made aware of such problems.

The main change in the present edition is that the scope has, with the help of co-authors, been much enlarged to extend beyond the limits of the Irish Sea. Jeremy Howard-Williams (former Managing Editor of Adlard Coles Limited) has undertaken to cover the Bristol Channel, while Bob Evans has described Milford Haven and the passage west along the south coast of Ireland. My own contribution, i.e. the whole of the Irish Sea, has been completely re-written with a great deal of the cultural and historical background material pruned away. This background may have made for readability, but a more concise format sharpens concentration on the job in hand. Corrections are up to Dec. 1982. From then onwards the yachtsman can take advantage of *Admiralty Notices to Mariners – Small Craft Edition*, published quarterly from 1979. My layout has been altered to make it more logical for visitors. Thus, the circumnavigation of the Irish Sea starts by departing from Milford Haven to make landfall at Rosslare on the south-east coast of Ireland, before heading north to Larne, across to Scotland at Stranraer and back again to Milford Haven, taking in the Isle of Man and Anglesey en passage. The south coast of Ireland then similarly starts from Milford Haven, goes across to Waterford Harbour, and proceeds west to Crookhaven. Finally, the Bristol Channel and adjacent waters also starts from Milford Haven, goes along the Welsh coast to Newport, and then jumps to St Ives to return to Bristol along the English coast.

In my view the current Admiralty charts are the best that the yachtsman has ever enjoyed, but it has to be remembered that large scale and full detail are only to be found in areas where there is active commercial traffic. To balance this, there are many more harbour plans, covering most of the ports likely to be entered by the sailing man. Both chart areas and chart numbers have been altered in the 1979 editions, and drying areas are carried down to lowest astronomical tide (LAT). As was foreshadowed in the first edition, there were new editions in 1978 for depths in metres and in 1979 for IALA buoyage, but the current charts should be longer lived. The present cost of the fifty charts needed to cover the whole of the Irish Sea is by no means cheap, but it would be a very long cruise that would call for them all at once. Yachtsmen tend to have human failings about charts even to the extent of disliking colouring, metres, and new buoyage. They can be heard saying that features and forces don't change and, even in a yacht costing tens of thousands of pounds, they can still be found clinging to trusted but out of date charts. We are particularly favoured in Liverpool in having the well-stocked chart agents of Dubois-Phillips and Macullum in the town. James Laver Ltd of Liverpool publish the best small tide tables for the Irish Sea based on Liverpool as the Standard Port, they also cover round the coast from seven other Standard Ports. The predictions come from Bidston in the Wirral.

As far as the writing and the reading of such a Cruising Guide or Pilot as this is concerned, it is to my mind unwise – even dangerous – to try to hold the skipper's hand too firmly. It has to be assumed that he can read a chart, plot a course, check his navigation by RDF, keep a log and analyse his mistakes. What the reader has to understand, is that the author is writing with his eye continuously on the latest corrected edition of the relevant chart drawn on the largest available scale. Since it would be a futile exercise to try to turn the chart back into words, it has to be assumed that the reader also has the proper chart under his eye as he reads. If not, then he will not understand the text which seeks only to supplement the already charted data. For this reason the chart number in use is placed at the head of each section.

Cruising in the context of the tough conditions of the Irish Sea and the Bristol Channel calls for a suitable boat. Fragile, tender, deep-keel boats cannot be the best choice, as there is a dearth of sheltered anchorages and moorings. Essentially a boat that can dry out and take the ground is needed to explore fully. The strong streams and high rise need good engine power. My own boat *Sarahay* has in long experience coped with the local problems. She has a closely fastened wooden hull with a long straight cast-iron keel supporting a powerful diesel engine. There is a small wheelhouse to keep one warm and dry, while there is a low aspect ketch rig. This is an old-fashioned prescription but is the answer to the rather basic cruising conditions under consideration.

The physical characteristics of the Irish Sea are those of a 200-mile long Sound, running on a north/south axis east of Ireland. Over such a large area the forecast must be a compromise, settling on the maximum weather likely to be found throughout this large expanse; local conditions can vary quite markedly within a range of fifty miles. From the yachtsman's point of view, it really needs to be divided into two sea areas on a line between Holyhead and Dublin Bay. The streams enter from both ends and meet in this area. The north-going flood, starting from the level of Carnsore Point, takes six hours to reach Liverpool and Dublin. An actual tidesmeet is found on either side of the Isle of Man; to the west is a streamless, but not tideless, zone. The south-going flood enters via the North Channel and manages to produce HW times uniformly throughout the northern half, all within half an hour of HW Liverpool. For simplicity it is best to use Liverpool tide tables throughout, these times are the same as those of Dover.

Tidal rises in the Irish Sea are on the high side, though not as high as those in the Bristol Channel. At Liverpool Pier Head the spring rise can be thirty-two feet (10m), even without the surge of a NW gale. The low rise of some five feet found round Arklow is an anomaly due to a nearby Amphidromic Centre. There is a nine feet higher rise in Liverpool Bay than in Caernarvon Bay on the other side of Anglesey. The winds are predominantly from the west, making Ireland the weather shore. A series of lows passing north of Scotland is the usual pattern linked with north-westerlies. The usual offshore stream rates do not rise beyond two knots but, off prominent land features such as the Mull of Galloway, the Isle of Man, Anglesey, Bardsey and St David's Head, the rates run up to five knots. In the narrow Sounds the rates can reach eight knots, for example in the Swellies and the Strangford Narrows. Thus the Irish Sea is no placid lake. The skipper/navigator will be fully extended in strategy, timing and tactics to make a good passage.

In nearly all my cruises and adventures I have been extremely lucky to have my friend and colleague, Mr Sam Davidson, to make a physician/surgeon team. We have endured the gales and enjoyed the good weather with never a cross word. Afloat, Sam ensures that the skipper makes a good landfall, then enjoys his landfall tot and praises the cook. Ashore, he polishes the image, glosses over my lack of tact, and manages to convey to the inquisitive a better impression than that of a couple of elderly doctors doddering round the Irish Sea. In addition I have been very much helped by, and am very grateful to, numerous Harbour Masters and Sailing Clubs who have replied to my enquiries as to recent local change; I understand that Bob Evans and Jeremy Howard-Williams are similarly indebted.

**Charts**

| No | Title | Scale 1: |
|---|---|---|
| 1121 | Irish Sea with St George's Channel and North Channel. | 500,000 |
| 1478 | St Govan's Head to St David's Head. | 75,000 |
| 1772 | Rosslare and Wexford Harbours with approaches. | 30,000 |
|  | Rosslare Harbour. | 10,000 |
| 1787 | Carnsore Point to Wicklow Head. | 100,000 |

**The Crossing**

Leaving Milford Haven via St Ann's Head and using Chart No 1478, the course could be either inside or outside Skokholm Island. Daylight is advisable if using Broad Sound in order to spot the overfalls charted. If going south of Skokholm, there should be a good clearance to avoid involvement with the Wild Goose Race. The next leg will be to the east of Grassholme in order not to get involved with the chain of rocks inside The Smalls. The N/S stream here will give a strong set, easing off as The Smalls come abeam. The marine radiobeacons on the South Bishop and The Smalls can be used to check the point of departure, from which a course can be laid for Rosslare, passing at least two miles north of Tuskar Rock to avoid overfalls; Tuskar itself has a marine radiobeacon. The traffic separation zones will be crossed at right angles but they will not normally be busy. The South Shear channel entry buoy – South Long – lies in the narrow white sector of the Rosslare harbour light. Rounding this the entrance is clear, but the harbour plan on Chart No 1772 needs careful study, because of recent improvements.

Rosslare is of characteristic railway engineer design and is sheltered only from north through east to south; yachts are exposed to any strong winds with an element of west in them. Thus there are no moorings, and the place is suitable only for short stay with a constant monitoring of the forecast. The anchoring-prohibited area shown on the chart has now been modified, so that the south boundary passes through the tip of the new pier. This is six hundred feet in length and has been constructed (presumably) to shelter the two Ro-Ro terminals at the base of the two piers. There is then plenty of room for anchoring outside the magenta pecked line in shallowing water. At the moment the No 1 berth at the new pier, i.e. the SW side, is available for yacht berthing. There is 5 to 7m (16.5–23 ft) of water for 25m (80 ft) from the wall. This is the exposed side, of course, the sheltered No 2 berth being used for ferry traffic. For any modifications of these arrangements, consult the Harbour Master at No 3 berth at the base of the old pier; there is a VHF harbour

1

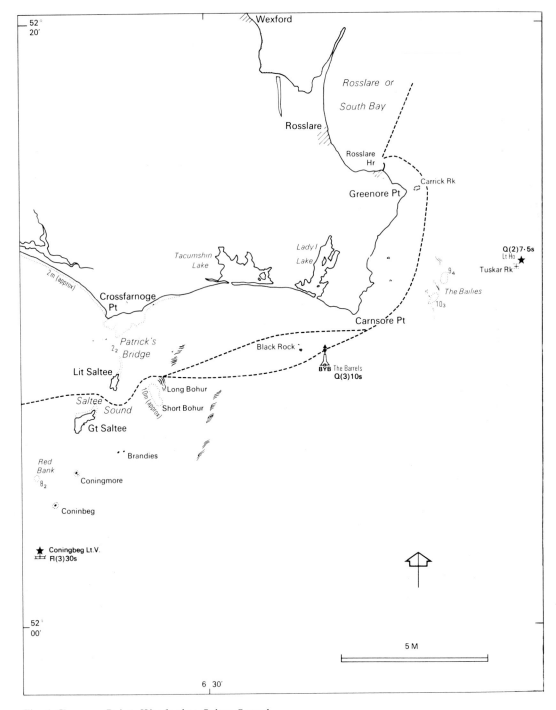

Fig. 1 Carnsore Point. Wexford to Saltee Sound.

2

*Rosslare.* The new pier had not been built when this photograph was taken; it now projects from where the photographer was standing. *Author*

radio link. There is a ship repair shop on Berth No 4, but otherwise the amenities and supplies ashore are rather limited.

The new pier had not been built when the accompanying illustrative photograph of Rosslare harbour was taken, but the pier has sprung from exactly this viewpoint. It is a great pity that harbour design, which no doubt appeared all right at the time, has proved so treacherous for yachts. For with the closure of Wexford, the siting is strategic for cruising, being midway between Arklow and Dunmore East – an overall distance of sixty rather difficult miles. There are problems arising from navigating inside the banks and juggling with the N/S axis streams.

**Charts**

| No | Title | Scale 1: |
|----|-------|----------|
| 633 | Plans on the east coast of Ireland: | — |
| | Arklow: Wicklow; Malahide inlet | 10,000 |
| | Skerries islands. | 12,500 |
| | Ardglass Harbour. | 15,000 |
| | Killough harbour; Rogerstown inlet. | 20,000 |
| 1411 | Irish Sea – western part. | 200,000 |
| 1415 | Dublin bay. | 25,000 |
| 1447 | Dublin and Dun Laoghaire: | — |
| | Port of Dublin; Dun Laoghaire harbour; Port of Dublin | |
| | entrance channel. | 7,500 |
| 1468 | Arklow to the Skerries islands. | 100,000 |
| 1772 | Rosslare and Wexford harbours with approaches. | 30,000 |
| | Rosslare harbour. | 10,000 |
| 1787 | Carnsore point to Wicklow head. | 100,000 |

**Wexford**

This is a sad story for yachtsmen, for Wexford offers good shelter if only a boat could get in. However, the shifting sands in the entry called for so much moving of the marks that the navigation was abandoned in the 1950's; it is used now only by a handful of fishing boats. I have heard of only one yacht going in, when the skipper persuaded a local boat to lead him. It may be possible to arrange for a pilot at Rosslare, and the data shown in Chart No 1772 suggests that there is water for entry, but the source shows that the last survey was many gales ago. There is no scarcity of quay berths near the bridge. Having turned its back on the sea, the town remains a bustling market town.

*The Irish Offshore Banks*

The essential chart is No 1787 as Chart No 1121 does not carry the full buoyage. In moving north from Carnsore Point or Rosslare it is possible to go outside the Banks, making a straight-forward long haul to Dublin Bay which does not call for any comment. The inshore passage is much more intriguing from the cruising point of view, with Arklow and Wicklow as ports of call. The Banks are a most remarkable phenomenon, as any skipper will agree after he has suddenly seen the seagulls walking six to eight miles out from the shore, and found himself aground within seconds. They stretch from Tuskar Rock to Lambay island, a distance of no

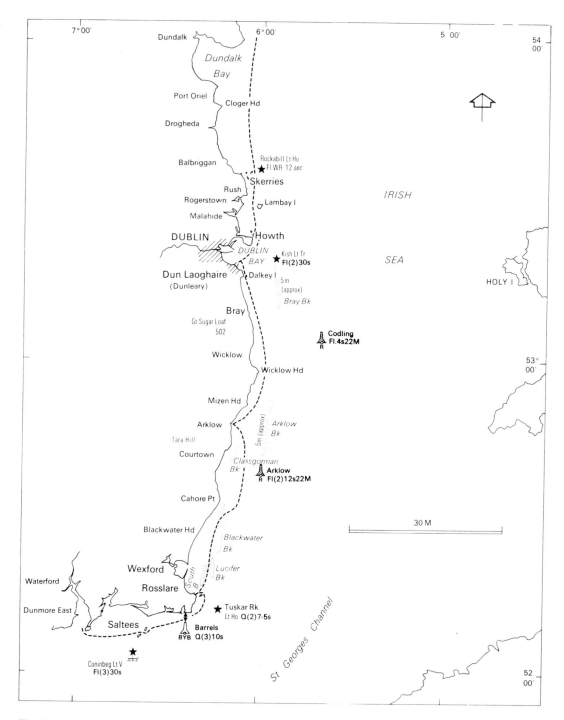

Fig. 2 Rosslare to Dublin. And north to Dundalk Bay.

5

less than eighty miles, and they are charted under a long list of different names. Parts of the Blackwater Bank actually dry and, though there is generally enough water for a yacht to cross, strong winds will set up some very rough water. Yet inside them there is a channel several miles wide in most places with an average least depth of forty feet (12m). I have never come across any attempt to explain the reasons for this long line of sandbanks.

The streams set along the coast for the most part, but cross the Banks diagonally. Outside they are charted up to four knots springs, while inside they are not shown at more than two knots. In practice, however, it is not easy to make much progress against them and, unless the boat is carrying the tide, it is often less frustrating to anchor inshore and await the change. In addition the tides are not balanced: in general terms the flow to the north runs for nine hours and the reversal for three hours. So that a yacht starting from Carnsore Point will have a favourable stream for much longer than one coming from Dublin Bay. This effect is enhanced by the fact that HW becomes progressively later as one goes north (HW at Tuskar is roughly six hours before Dublin). As can be seen by this oversimplified explanation, the navigator is going to be stretched to work out the timing of the inshore passage; he will also find that it is necessary to have clear visibility to pick up the next buoy. It is vital to pick up and read each buoy on the passage list, otherwise it is quite possible to cross a bank inadvertently and find oneself on the wrong side. Should this happen, the advice is to stay there until there is a clear opportunity to regain the proper course.

### Rosslare to Arklow

The north-bound passage is simple, merely a matter of starting at low water. On the passage from Arklow in the reverse direction, the thirty-five mile trip is likely to run out of time without anything better than an open bay such as Polduff to pull into for anchorage; there is no intermediate harbour. Having a powerful engine, my method is to set out from Arklow with about four hours flood (preferably at neaps), the simple elegance of pure sailing is at a discount over this piece of ground. Unfortunately the Rusk Channel and the buoys inside the Blackwater Bank are unlit, and it would be necessary to go outside at night.

Leaving Rosslare then, the North Shear channel holds inside the Long Bank with the low-lying sandy coast of the Wexford entry hardly to be made out. The West Long buoy lies three miles on, and North Long buoy another three miles – both reasonably easy to find; the West Blackwater buoy (small green conical) is five miles ahead and out of sight. The S Blackwater buoy now lies to seaward and is to be ignored. Blackwater Head is inshore of the West Blackwater buoy, but is hardly distinguishable from the rest of the coast. Rusk No 1 and No 2 buoys three miles ahead should be visible, and they mark the entry to the Rusk Channel; passing between Rusk Bank and Money-weights Bank, this extends for three miles to Rusk No 4 and on to Rusk No 6. None of the Rusk buoys is lit, nor are they IALA. The N Blackwater is IALA pattern and is left to seaward.

6

At this stage Cahore Point is clearly defined, but the trees are growing to hide Cahore House; Polduff village just beyond can be made out with charted anchorage off. The next buoy is Glassgorman No 1, which is seven miles ahead and out of sight, calling for a compass course, though the stream is right aft. Courtown lies five miles to shoreward of Glassgorman No 1 and can generally be identified with anchorage-off charted. There is a harbour here, but the entry may be undredged and not give enough water. Owing to the presence of an inland Amphidromic Centre the tidal rise is only a few feet, which hardly helps. The dominating landmark at this stage is the sugarloaf outline of Tara Hill. It should be noted that in charts since 1979 the direction of buoyage has altered; what is now Glassgorman No 1 was G3, while this latter buoy has been withdrawn. The Arklow lightship has also gone, its place having been taken by a high focal light buoy five miles to seaward of Glassgorman No 1.

The last buoy (Glassgorman No 1) is five miles to the north of No 2. By this time Kilmichael Point can be identified and Arklow can be clearly seen ahead.

The orthodox inside-the-banks passage just described is the usual one taken by yachts because it is marked and charted, because there is no real intermediate harbour and because of the illusion that the Banks will give outside shelter. This part of the coast is indeed rather flat and uninteresting, but it is the weather coast for the prevalent westerlies and thus gives smooth water for sailing. If the weather is fresh offshore it should, of course, be possible to crawl round the coast keeping close in, keeping inside Glassgorman and Rusk Banks and following the 5m line. The stream would be slacker inshore and when it turns against there are charted anchorages close in.

### Arklow

Use the plan in Chart No 633. There is no direct approach from the east, because of the Arklow Bank which is buoyed at both ends and has two seaward buoys. The Bank dries at the north end, but in settled weather there will be enough water for a

*Arklow.* Commercial activity in the approach by the Avoca river. The crumbling walls have now been rebuilt. *Author*

yacht to cross further to the south; with any strength of wind it should be carefully circumvented. The nearer approaches to Arklow are clear and recognition easy. The bar has always been a problem, and the peat-stained ebb from the River Avoca can be seen – though it is now well dredged, strong onshore winds may play it up. The harbour, which was until a few years ago much run down, has recently been completely rebuilt and the dock has been dredged to 3m (10 ft). The rise and fall is the lowest recorded round these coasts, with a rise and fall in the dock of three to six feet at extremes. This, added to the fact that the dock is completely sheltered from all directions, makes it a snug berth.

Though the harbour is narrow, fair-sized trading ships come in and it is busy commercially. Turning these ships and threading them through the narrow dock entrance will necessarily hold up yachts. The Tyrell boatyard occupies the top end of the dock, but elsewhere there is room for yachts in tiers; there is also yacht berthing at the walls above the dock entry. The town is enjoyable and there are full supplies and services. Many of us have happy memories of a stay in Arklow. It is so unusual to rest in a completely protected harbour with the added bonus of having no warps to tend.


### Wicklow

See plan in Chart No 633. The eleven-mile leg from Arklow to Wicklow is straight-forward with the flood stream astern. There is smooth sailing keeping about two miles offshore. The coast is low and featureless, so that Mizzen Head is difficult to make out. When passing inside Arklow Bank, it is as well to remember that there are no inshore buoys and no buoy for the close-in Wolf Rock. A mile short of Wicklow Head lighthouse, the Horseshoe Rock Buoy should be located and best left to port. If there is any wind, it may well be advisable to give the Head a berth of at least a mile, to avoid the rough water that is generally to be found over the reefs off-lying. On the Head itself, the upper two disused towers have been left as landmarks, with the new house nearly at sea level to avoid cloud cover. Having rounded, the harbour can be seen two miles to the NW; there is open entry between the two pier heads.

The harbour is well protected except for the sector from NW to NE and northerly gales come straight in, so that the forecasts have to be routinely monitored. From the NW there is shelter at anchor under the West Pier and from the NE at the East Pier, but the latter is rough and calls for barge boards. In settled weather most yachts anchor in the main harbour off the sands. My own preference is to go up the river and find a berth at the Packet Quay. Generally it is possible to lie afloat here, but the river shoals quickly and, if a loose cargo is being unloaded nearby, there may be dust; shelter is however good with perhaps a little swell. There is some commercial traffic as at Arklow, but little trawler work.

The town is close at hand with good supplies and services, with trains to Dublin. The sailing club is particularly helpful and hospitable.

8

*Dalkey Island.* Dalkey Sound is between the harbour and the island, with the Mugglins beacon showing to the left. *Author*

### Wicklow to Dublin Bay

This leg of twenty miles is simple weather shore sailing. The series of off-lying banks continues: India, Codling, and Kish, with the stream tending to cross them diagonally. They are however well buoyed, though again mostly along the outer side. Heading north from Wicklow it is important to locate the small Breaches buoy seven miles away, and pass outside it, and do the same with the Moulditch buoy two miles further on. The green cone buoy to the west of Codling, three miles further east, might well be sighted and left to starboard. The resorts of Greystones, Bray and Killiney have only small boat harbours and no shelter for yachts, except anchorage off. After Bray Head, Sorrento Terrace on the entry point, Dalkey Island and Muglins present. Dalkey Sound (Chart No 1415) offers a deep clear passage and can be followed close inshore. Dalkey harbour (see photograph and marked Coliemore on chart) is a small boat harbour, as is Bullock harbour higher up. Sometimes a line of floats crosses the fairway, these are starter marks. Within sighting distance now, the entry to Dunleary Harbour can be seen.

### *Dun Laoghaire (Dunleary) Harbour*

There is a wide clear entry but an eye has to watch for car ferries coming up astern or leaving harbour. They may pivot either outside or inside the harbour, reversing all flags and lights. There are several possibilities for berthing a yacht:

1. Anchoring is banned in the area of Fairways No 1 and No 2.
2. The anchorage lies in the triangle between the two Fairways.
3. The moorings in the angle of the East Pier are those of the Royal St George and National Clubs – clubhouses ashore.
4. The Royal Irish YC have their mooring trots in front of the clubhouse. The best ploy is to pick up a vacancy in the outer trots and go ashore for a yarn with the club boatman.

9

*Dunleary.* The Royal Irish Yacht Club from the moorings. *Author*

5. Moorings in the crook of the West Pier are mostly privately laid.

6. The inner, or coal, harbour was opened in 1827. There is not a great depth of water and vacant moorings will be scarce. It is usually possible to find a floating berth at Traders' Wharf. This is convenient but a boat cannot be left unattended here and, with a NE gale, a circular scend comes in.

7. The Old Harbour almost dries and is full of small boat moorings, with the clubhouse of the Dunleary Motor YC on the quay. Here the shelter is absolute.

Dunleary is very similar to its railway-engineered twin at Holyhead. Generally it is well sheltered and sunny, and was completed about 1840. As at Holyhead however, there is the same fatal gap in the defences due to the wide sailing ship entrance, which allows gales and swell to come in from a wide NE arc. What is badly needed is an extension to the east wall to protect the entrance; there would then be room for a large marina under the West wall. The current plan is, however, to build a marina for two hundred boats in front of the National YC, as this site has now become available.

When heavy weather is forecast from the NE, berths on the RIYC trots are uncomfortable, though the ground tackle is very heavy. The first thing for the visitor living aboard to do in such a case, is to see that the wire mooring strop is lashed firmly into the fairleads; if the strop jumps out there may well be a chain-saw effect, and I have seen one hull cut down to the water line in this way. The next thing to do

*Kish Bank Tower.* Elusive in the mist, with faint RDF signals. (Range still only 20 miles.) *Author*

is to go ashore for the night; alternatively the boat could be taken into the Liffey. It is well said that a yacht would be better off at sea than in Dunleary in a NE gale.

It is well that Dunleary comes early in our circuit of the Irish Sea, for it is extremely civilised and hitherto the most prestigious yachting centre – though within a year or two Howth will be a strong rival. The waterline is attractive, the wind usually offshore and the launch service good. Ashore the three yacht clubs are gems of Victorian genre from which many visitors have received much hospitality. The town too has changed little since partition (except for the colour of the pillar boxes). Supplies and services are excellent as is the chandlery (Perrys) in the High Street. The railway runs along the coast from Dublin to Bray and was once pneumatically operated. There is a frequent bus service to and from O'Connell Bridge. In all, one could be well satisfied merely to cruise to Dunleary and take a holiday there.

Perhaps Dunleary's prime asset is as a base to explore Dublin itself. The Horse Show, the galleries and museums, and particularly the history of the last sixty years, are obvious attractions (the Holy Hour lasts from 1400 to 1600 hours daily). It is best to take a supply of Punta (Irish pounds), though more can be easily raised on a Banker's card. Car hire requires a driving licence and certificate of insurance. The political climate should be sampled very discreetly and ensigns with the Union flag never flown afloat or ashore. Politics apart (and remember that the native will always triumph in any discussion), everybody is endlessly helpful and reassuring.

It is to be understood that the Republic of Ireland is technically a foreign country and Dunleary a port of entry. Thus form C1328 (Pleasure craft UK based) should be prepared in advance and Customs clearance obtained on entry.

*The River Liffey*

The existence of such a fine plan of the river as is shown in Chart No 1447 is in itself a plea for exploration. Not that this could be labelled yachting, which is carried on at the three Dublin outports of Dunleary, Howth and Malahide. One must not be put off by the colour of the water as it passes through the city. This is a suspension of grey clay and peat – not sewage as is often suggested. There is no strong current in the river as it does not drain from an upstream lagoon – merely a tidal rise and fall of about twenty feet. The only surprise packet is the Liverpool hydrofoil which, if it is running, can come up astern at a speed of twenty knots, though there is no wash. Wash is however a danger to yachts using the main channel from No 1 Bar buoy, as ships move through at high speeds. The usual yacht approach will however be from Dunleary to the twin lighthouses of Poulbeg and North Bull. The Great South Wall is obvious enough but the N Bull Wall covers, and skippers must resist the temptation to pass inside the lighthouse. Thus at HW the lower end of the channel is still exposed to the E and NE, from which the boat may be hoping to shelter. There is however water for yachts at all states up to the first road bridge.

Above the lighthouses, the channel is dredged and well buoyed; the centre of commercial activity has moved seaward from the city leaving the centre rather derelict. The various activities are clearly charted but it is doubtful that yachts would be accepted into the dock system. The only moorings to be met with are on the south bank below the Dodder Buoy. These are privately laid and of unknown quality but, since there is little commercial traffic above this point, anchorage off this reach might be considered.

The Dodder buoy marks the entry of the Dodder which is not navigable. Here too Ringsend Quay turns in at right angles to the south wall. It offers a sheltered berth afloat with a rise and fall of about twenty feet and a set of slippery steps; on the opposite bank is a scrap yard with patrol dogs. A few local fishing boats use the quay higher up and supply the river information. Yachts have no permanent berths here for, despite the Docks Police, the blighted area smells of vandalism if not piracy. However *Sarahay* spent a comfortable night here in a NE gale. There is now no commercial or trawler traffic.

At the top of the quay are the entry locks to the Grand Canal system which, when in repair, is reputed navigable to the west coast. The three locks have engraved in the granite: *Westmoreland Dock 1790*; one remains in use but a permit is needed to pass it. The lock opens into the vast, L-shaped and empty Grand Canal Dock. What a handy marina this would make – just the place to fit out for a world cruise, and good training for the hostile tribes likely to be met en route.

Above the Dodder buoy, both the north and the south wall are quayed, with occasional sets of steps but little commerce. There is a good view of the Customs

House, which was burnt during the Troubles, but the cast iron skeleton survived; it has since been re-built to its former glory. At the top of the south wall, just below the road bridge, is the Guinness Quay and the home berths of the ships of the Irish Lights service. Hereabouts there are steps at which one can tie up in the centre of the city. A boat cannot however be left safely without a watchkeeper, and at night should be pulled away from the steps.

The return journey down river should be without incident unless there is strong wind in the Bay, in which case the short leg from Poulbeg to Dunleary can be pretty rough. When lying in Dunleary with a poor forecast from the south, the shelter under the land may be deceptive enough to tempt a skipper out. By making a short jaunt through Dalkey Sound one can easily see what effect the wind over the ebb is having out to sea. Under the same conditions there will be some rough going round the Nose of Howth. Rather than spending the time swinging on the buoy, a trip up the Liffey is a good alternative.

## Howth

Use Chart No 1415 – Dublin Bay, there is no plan and the topography is in the process of radical alteration with the re-building of the harbour. Howth Sound (pronounced Hoath) is shown in Chart No 1468, as is Lambay Island. The short seven mile trip from Dunleary seems clear enough, but in practice produces a

*Howth Harbour.* Note the trawlers' wash skirting the small buoy off the rocks under the east pierhead. Ireland's Eye is in the background. *Author*

built-in hazard. On many of the occasions that I have tried to pass close under the cliffs of the Ben of Howth in any but calm weather, it was to meet very rough seas off the Nose. Thus it is best in any wind to keep a mile or even two to the east, and not turn until the harbour is well open. In reverse on leaving, the rough conditions at the Nose can be seen with glasses from the sea wall, in which case an initial course should be laid on the Rowan Rocks buoy (IALA) before turning east.

The story of Howth is that it was built as a terminal for the sailing packets in about 1820 but, though the entrance was sheltered by Ireland's Eye, most of the harbour area was shown to dry to solid rock, and an alternative had to be started at Dunleary. In more recent years part of the harbour has been cleared by underwater blasting. The present scheme is nothing less than the complete excavation of the whole harbour area at an initial cost of eight million punta; completion will be half way through the eighties. The plans include a trawler basin, a fish market, a clubhouse in the centre, and a large marina.

The end result will be a large harbour with complete shelter and deep water throughout, in other words the leading yachting centre for the Irish Sea. Until the changes are completed there will be very few berths available for visitors, but the club boatman may be able to find a temporary mooring on the trots outside. I have been into Howth on many occasions previously and always been very welcome; during the 1981 season the harbour works were well under way. On the pier there is a good supply of fish, all services and supplies and a touch of night life at the shoreward end. The village lies on high ground behind the harbour, and Dublin is reached both by road and rail, while there is plenty of walking exercise on the Ben. The gun-running by Erskine Childers in 1914 is commemorated by a plaque on the east wall, while the veritable Asgard lies in Kilmainham Gaol.

**Charts**

| No | Title | Scale 1: |
|----|-------|----------|
| 44 | Howth to Ardglass. | 100,000 |
| 633 | Plans on the east coast of Ireland: | — |
| | Arklow: Wicklow; Malahide inlet. | 10,000 |
| | Skerries islands. | 12,500 |
| | Ardglass harbour. | 15,000 |
| | Killough harbour; Rogerstown inlet. | 20,000 |
| 1411 | Irish Sea – western part. | 200,000 |
| 1415 | Dublin Bay. | 25,000 |
| 1423 | Dundalk and approaches. | 20,000 |
| 1431 | River Boyne to Drogheda. | 10,000 |
| 1468 | Arklow to the Skerries islands. | 100,000 |
| 2800 | Carlingford Lough. | 20,000 |
| | Kilkeel harbour. | 5,000 |
| | Warrenpoint. | 10,000 |
| | Entrance to Carlingford Lough. | 12,500 |

**Malahide Inlet**

See plan in Chart No 633. This is the third of the Dublin outports and is quiet and unpretentious. Lying three miles north of Ireland's Eye, the approach is rather deceptive. The topography is that of a large inland lagoon, the emptying of which scours the channel below the railway bridge and across the sand delta. The first thing to note is that the stream table and diamond refer to a point well offshore; in the channel the current is much stronger and the ebb prolonged. The chart suggests a direct approach from the east, but this is unwise for the south bank is building a spit; the safer way is to come down from the north following the shore, which is now built up (making the Martello tower hard to pick out). Before venturing in, the two temporary buoys should be located, using the charted bearing on the Chapel spire. At half flood the channel, which is unbuoyed, is fairly evident and has sufficient water for small craft. From the inner buoy the town should be clear enough along the straight channel.

Off the town there are moorings, which sometimes have a vacancy; it is best to pick up and make enquiries at the club ashore (there is a good slip). Anchorage is higher up towards the bridge and the bottom foul with old moorings. The boatyard is mainly at work converting trawlers and there may be a mooring off. The harbour

15

is well sheltered except from an easterly gale. The town itself is a quiet little gem fifteen miles by bus from Dublin, and supplies and services are good; Dublin airport is a taxi ride away with its aerobeacon further north at Rush.

### Lambay Island

This is best charted on Chart No 44, but is also covered by numbers 1468 and 1411. Lying about five miles north of Ireland's Eye, yachts would normally pass inside it on courses to and from Howth. By day it is obvious enough, being steep sided and one and half miles across, with two unlit beacons on the inshore side. On the mainland coast there are no lights, apart from those of Rush airport (with aerobeacon), thus it is rather surprising to note that the island itself has no lighthouse; a night passage would therefore call for a course east of the Kish-Rockabill line, or homing onto Rockabill in its white sector.

The island is privately owned and is a bird sanctuary, landing not usually being allowed. The charted small harbour is again private with mainland contact at Rogerstown. To the east Lambay is steep-to with anchorage possible only close in. In practice there is no shelter, but on a calm day one can lie in Salt Pan Bay or the Seal Hole or find shallower water to the west. I have never had any success in fishing, but the ornithologist will have a good opportunity to study a wide variety of sea birds. The island makes an interesting circumnavigation, but the inability to land is frustrating and after a while the tendency is to push on towards Rockabill.

### Rogerstown Inlet

See plan in Chart No 633; approaches in Chart No 1468. I have no personal experience of this harbour which lies two and a half miles west of Lambay Island. The little bay is marked on either hand by a Martello Tower, and has Rush aerobeacon centrally placed but too close to be of much help. There is no fairway buoy, though the channel across the sands may be locally perched. A course should be laid on the pier and the echo sounder used to come in on the flood. The pier dries out, but should give absolute shelter from the east and there will be water enough to float in the channel. As with Malahide, there is an inland lagoon to scour the channel.

Just to the north of Rogerstown is the village of Rush. Here there is a well built stone pier used by fishing boats. It dries to the tip but gives complete shelter from most directions except north. There are no lights or beacons but, by coming in after half flood and berthing alongside before taking the ground, a suitable yacht will do well here, though there are no yachting facilities as such.

### The Skerries Islands

See Chart No 1468 and a fully detailed plan in Chart No 633. Lying about six miles north of Lambay Island, with Rockabill lighthouse three miles off shore, the islands offer a miniature cruising ground on a leisurely holiday; fair weather and clear visibility are however needed – I once spent two nights and three days fogbound and

16

lost off the shore a few miles to the north and only got away, still in fog, by homing in on Rockabill's four blast foghorn. Given the plan in Chart No 633 there are several sheltered anchorages among the islands, though these are not charted. Alternatively it is possible to win round to Skerries Bay, the course being both buoyed and lit, where there is good shelter from the east (but not from the north) given by Red Island, now a holiday camp; there is anchorage in the bay where one can lie afloat well tucked in – better still is to come alongside the good stone wall and dry out with absolute shelter. As always the most interesting parts of cruising in the Irish Sea are open only to a boat that can comfortably take the ground. The town is fully supplied and welcoming.

**Balbriggan**
See Chart No 1468 (there is no plan on Chart No 633). This is a small quite old harbour with on the one hand complete shelter but on the other it is tidal and silted. Lying three miles NW of the Skerries harbour it is located by the prominent beacon on the Cardy Rocks to the north and the outstanding light tower at the end of the wall. The entry is tricky in easterly onshore winds, which may make getting in and getting out impossible; the last part of the run in is parallel with the shore onto which a boat could be swept. The outer wall is lit and the light sectored.

*Balbriggan*. A tricky entry in onshore winds. *Author*

**Drogheda**

For approach use Chart No 44; the plan of Drogheda port (pronounced Drocheda) has now been turned into Chart No 1431. From this it will be seen that the harbour lies five miles from the Fairway buoy, across a flat and marshy delta traversed by the River Boyne of historic note; a conspicuous landmark is the power station with its chimneys. It should be said at once that the port is purely commercial and has almost no yachting facilities, but there is complete shelter and it offers an interesting exploration. In easterly weather the very definite bar makes it a place to run for before the gale has developed and before the ebb has set in. As can be seen there is ample provision of lit beacons from the Fairway onwards for ship traffic, and the channel has sufficient water for yachts at most states of the tide. The channel has however little room for anchorage either side if big ships are to pass. The main activity now is the import of coal which is landed at the power station and the town quays. For channel one might almost read canal, the width varying from five hundred down to two hundred yards. This means that ships will not be able to slow or alter and that yachts will find sailing almost impossible and will have to manoeuvre under engine.

A yacht presses on up the long and monotonous channel until the harbour is heralded by the high-level and very ugly railway bridge. It is just possible to lie afloat at anchor near the south bank but it should be possible, by negotiation with the Harbour Master, to find a berth at the quay; the walls, however, are crumbling and dirty so that a yacht would best tie up outside another boat. It is very much a case of any port in a storm, but no doubt some of the good points of the place have escaped my notice.

*Drogheda*. A view which shows the industrial setting. *Author*

**Port Oriel**

See Chart No 44. There is no plan and the topography is simple enough not to call for one. Clogher Head stands out, being five miles north of Drogheda and a similar distance south of Dunany Point; Port Oriel is just inside Clogher Head. There is no yachting activity here, no moorings and no anchorage; nor indeed is it a harbour. It simply functions as the base for a handful of trawlers, which will probably multiply now that the fish processing factory is completed. Despite this, with a satisfactory slant of the wind it offers a deep water berth for a cruising yacht to stay over-night. The stout stone pier (which is unlit) heads north, giving good shelter from NE round to SW, but open particularly from the NW. When I was last there, a gale sprang up from this quarter and we had to clear out hurriedly, cross Dundalk Bay, and sit it out in Kilkeel. In settled weather, however, it is possible to tie up to the wall above the trawlers in comfort since there is deep water to the shoreward end. It is best to keep a low political profile and see that any ensign with the Union flag is kept in the locker.

Insurance against the known exposure is provided by an inner tidal dock which is boomed off when needed with timber baulks. Here a yacht can dry out in safety if necessary, though exit may be delayed. The local atmosphere is friendly and the

*Port Oriel.* The wall has water to its shoreward end. *Author*

Harbour Master helpful, but there are no facilities at the harbour; these are to be found in the village about half a mile away across lush countryside. In the high street there is the most concentrated collection of pubs likely to be seen anywhere.

### Dundalk

For approaches use Chart No 44, and for entry Chart No 1423 is essential. The harbour lies in the NW corner of Dundalk Bay and its entrance crosses the sands. The town is about six miles from the green IALA fairway buoy, and indications for entry are much the same as for Drogheda. There is shelter at the top of a long winding channel, but little other advantage from the point of view of yachting; the navigation is maintained for small coastal trading vessels and some offshore fishing boats. A yacht comes in across shallowing water and has to negotiate a tricky, shifting and exposed bar. It is really something for settled offshore weather rather than one to run for as shelter from an easterly gale, for if entry were not possible then the boat would be on a lee shore. However given Chart No 1423, proper conditions and a rising tide, it is possible to motor up to Dundalk as the channel is very well marked and maintained. At Dundalk there are sheltered berths at the quays though most will dry out. The town itself is self-sufficient and pleasant.

### Lough Carlingford

The Lough was previously charted on two sheets, but the current Chart No 2800 is on one sheet with inset plans of Kilkeel and Warrenpoint. This chart is essential and shows a miniature cruise of both maritime and political interest.

The immediate question raised is that of the border between the Republic and Northern Ireland. Crews may be reluctant to cross the line in the present circumstances, while customs and entry have to be arranged. For convenience, entry to Northern Ireland may be made at Kilkeel and the Lough penetrated later when the tide serves. Even so there is the question of dodging across the line for harbourage. The line runs down the middle of the Lough and is so shown on the road map, but there is no line on the chart nor any buoyed border. There is a similar situation in Lough Foyle to the north, where the site of the first sabotaged collier is still a matter of dispute, while a second ship has been sunk close to the southern side (for insurance purposes, it is probably best to sink well to the north of the line in Carlingford). The Royal Navy patrols the offshore three mile limits and will probably challenge and search yachts. In the Lough itself there is usually an RN trawler at anchor for the purpose of challenging passing yachts. There seems to be no reciprocal Republican naval presence south of the border. These are the arrangements at the time of writing, but they may alter at any time.

If coasting, the approach is clear enough between Ballagan Point and Cranfield Point. If coming from the Isle of Man, the high background is not easy to sort out and there is no RDF beacon. Carlingford entrance lies between the Carlingford Mountain to the south and the Mountains of Mourne to the north; both are likely to be hidden by rain or mist. The dominant landmark is the prominent weathered bulk

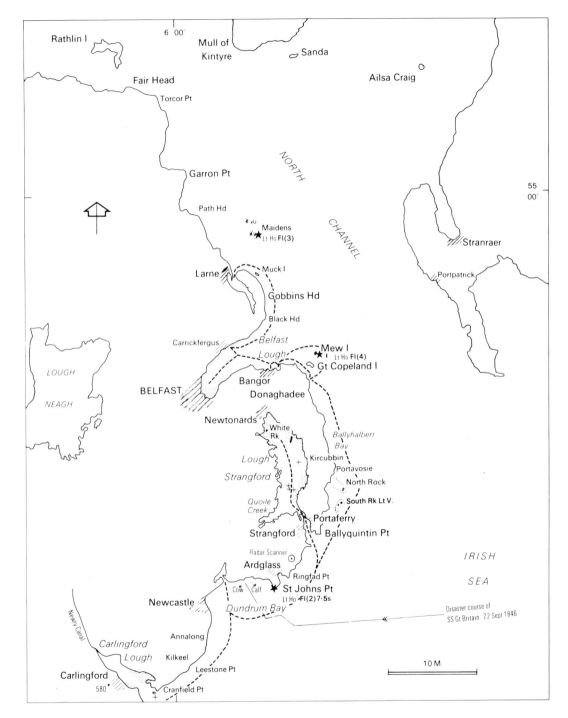

Fig. 3 Carlingford Lough to Larne. With Stranraer.

21

of the Haulbowline lighthouse drawing one in from many miles to seaward. Only the most adventurous would think of entering south of the lighthouse by using the Hoskyn Channel, which is now completely unmarked over the sands and between the rocks. On the north side and using the Carlingford Cut, there is a clear well-marked channel suitable for quite large ships up to Warrenpoint. There is a strong stream, charted up to 4½ knots, which may deny entry for yachts in onshore winds, while passage should always be made with the tide.

The charted marks look rather involved, but in the event all falls easily into place when actually making the passage. The buoys are all lit allowing a night entry, but apart from the Hellyhunter, they are simple cans and cones. Having located the Hellyhunter, the leading line (True from seaward) carries one through to the first dogleg – a distance of two miles. From close-to the lighthouse looks even more elderly and its narrow fixed red sector gives the signal to alter for the dogleg. Beyond buoys Nos 5 and 6, the stream eases off and the course heads away to the Republican side and passes close to Grenore. It might be said that the inlet begins to open up but, unless it is a sunny day, the high land each side and the frequent rain gives a gloomy cast to the scene. It is also a reminder that gales from the NW are all too capable of sweeping down the length of the Lough. The scenery is of course marvellous. The following harbours and anchorages are available within the Lough.

1. *Behind Green Island*. The plan of entrance shows a charted anchorage in the pool and near the slipway. Here there is deep water and a certain amount of shelter from the north, though isolated and devoid of home comforts; there are however moorings privately laid.

2. *Greenore*. Since this harbour is on the Republican side I have not been in, but from the chart it seems satisfactory. It boasts a full breakwater facing NW, with room to anchor between this and the harbour wall with sufficient water to lie afloat.

3. *Carlingford*. Here the harbour dries completely, but the approach is clear though not buoyed. Two piers give a good deal of shelter except from directly north, otherwise anchorage off is open to a fairly wide arc.

4. *Rostrevor*. There are moorings here and a yacht club; between the quay and Killowen there is a certain amount of shelter.

5. *Warrenpoint*. This is probably the best centre to aim for, following the buoyed deep channel. With the closure of the Newry navigation, this harbour has built up to a small modern port transhipping in and out of Northern Ireland without crossing the border. Apart from the port development, a new breakwater has been built to the east. Inside this, trots have been laid and a floating stage, which cater both for visitors and local boat owners. While it cannot rate as a marina, it is sheltered and reasonably secure; there is anchorage out of the big ship fairway on the other side of the breakwater. Boats can dry out in the Town Dock from which a ferry crosses to the opposite shore at Omeath. The town of Warrenpoint is quiet but self sufficient. The surrounding country is attractive though recent tragic events would not encourage tourism.

**Charts**

| No | Title | Scale 1: |
|---|---|---|
| 44 | Howth to Ardglass. | 100,000 |
| 633 | Plans on the east coast of Ireland: | — |
| | Arklow: Wicklow; Malahide inlet. | 10,000 |
| | Skerries islands. | 12,500 |
| | Ardglass harbour. | 15,000 |
| | Killough harbour: Rogerstown inlet. | 20,000 |
| 1237 | Larne Lough and approaches. | 10,000 |
| 1411 | Irish Sea – western part. | 200,000 |
| 1753 | Belfast Lough. | 37,500 |
| | Belfast docks. | 12,500 |
| | Bangor Bay. | 17,500 |
| 2156 | Strangford Lough. | 37,500 |
| 2198 | North Channel – southern part. | 75,000 |
| 2800 | Carlingford Lough. | 20,000 |
| | Kilkeel harbour. | 5,000 |
| | Warrenpoint. | 10,000 |
| | Entrance to Carlingford Lough. | 12,500 |
| 3709 | Copeland islands and Donaghadee Sound. | 12,500 |

**Kilkeel**

For approaches see Chart No 44; the plan of the harbour is in Chart No 2800. Until 1974 this harbour was decayed and silted by the Kilkeel river which ran through it; it was then completely rebuilt as an important trawler base. It is not a yachting centre though there are some smaller boats with berths there. For the cruising yacht it is a safe and secure harbour of refuge with Customs and Entry facilities. Lying four miles north of the Haulbowline Lt Ho, there is a background of the Mourne Mountains. With an eight mile light on the breakwater, its identification and location is not difficult except in heavy rain, but there are no off-lying buoys. It is clean and new, with the entrance so designed that little if any of an easterly gale comes in, and in particular there is no bar so that one can run to it in safety. A gale from the the NW, however, sweeps down from the mountains and comes strongly into the back of the harbour, and yachts should be moored with this in mind.

From the plan it can be seen that there is a well-guarded but unobstructed entry, signalled by trawlers moving in and out like bees to a hive. There is water for yachts

*Kilkeel*. Clinically clean, with ample water, quay space and ladders. *Author*

at all states, with a rise and fall of ten to fifteen feet. The entrance to the Inner Harbour is narrow, angled and blind so that it is best not to meet a trawler at this spot. Trawlers line the quay to port, and the best ploy is to tie up temporally outside one and go across to the Harbour Master's Office to report entry. He will probably direct a yacht to the top of the harbour near the area marked Spending Beach where the smaller boats lie; it is wise to put out independent mooring lines. With heavy rain in the hills the Kilkeel river overflows into the dock, and this has already produced silting though not sufficient to affect yachts, which remain afloat. The quays and the nearby village provide all supplies, but it has to be remembered that the Irish punt may now be at a discount.

Yachts will not be particularly popular in an active trawler harbour, so that a certain amount of suave PR work will not be out of place. Nearness to the border means that both camps are well represented and a very low political profile is by far the best. However fishing and going to sea cannot work out in ideological terms, and I gathered that public opinion was firmly against anything that might interfere with the harmony of running the harbour – though the slogans on the wall of the iceplant did seem a little one-sided.

**Analong**

Use Chart No 44 (there is no harbour plan). Situated five miles north of Kilkeel, this little harbour has a five-mile light but otherwise is not easy to pick out except when coasting close in. It is at the mouth of the Analong river, with an old water mill on the north bank which has recently been restored. This is a well-loved resort of the week-end cruiser, but is very quiet during the week and quite a haven for the longer distance cruising man. There will be difficulty in getting in with heavy onshore weather but there are no off-lying hazards. Almost immediately on entry there is a right angled turn to port through a narrow opening, which can be boomed off to exclude swell. The basin is small and silted, and dries early. Thus there is no local yachting fleet and it is mainly used by fishing boats, the catches being salted or kippered nearby. There is a good local atmosphere (added to by the kippering) and the harbour is very old; there is plenty of evidence of this in the delightful quayside pub. The drill is to come in near the top of the tide and settle down comfortably on the soft mud.

Having described the small harbour as it has been for so many years, there is now a proposal for rebuilding, so that hopefully within a few years we may see a design planned for inshore fishing boats and deep keel yachts.

**Dundrum Bay**

See Chart No 44. This shallow bay has an open easterly exposure and lies between the northerly end of the Mourne Mountains (where they go down to the sea) and St John's Point, with little yachting interest. The seaside resort of Newcastle has only a small boat harbour, which is dry for long periods and is unsuitable for drying out for this reason. There two deep water anchorages charted along the coast to the north suitable in offshore winds. St John's Pt lighthouse is an important mark for yachts sailing directly from the south. It is unusually banded in yellow and black like a wasp, and stands at the tip of a bleak rocky promontory (see aerial photograph); there is a powerful Gp (2) flash. The two jutting ports on its tower are for fixed sectorised lights to guard against ships standing into the bay. On the 22nd of September 1846 the *SS Great Britain* did just this, on passage from Liverpool to New York. The navigator under-assessed her speed (it has been done before and since) and in the dark evidently failed to see the Calf at the Isle of Man, and mistook St John's Point for it – an error of some 40 miles. Turning starboard with the intention of passing through the North Channel into the Atlantic, he put the ship firmly but gently on the shelving sands of Dundrum Bay, between the Cow and Calf rocks, from which undignified position she was salvaged with little damage save to reputation.

*Dundrum*

Chart No 44 (there is no harbour plan). The entry is marked by a yellow spoil buoy and a fairway buoy, but both are unlit; the channel is charted as being marked by posts and buoys. Most of the harbour dries out, but it is accessible to yachts.

*St John's Point*. The lighthouse seen from the SW. *Author*

*Ardglass*. Anchor between the pierhead and the mid-harbour beacon. In the background can be seen the old quay with God's Pocket. *Author*

*Killough Harbour*

See Chart No 44; the place has been accorded a harbour plan in Chart No 633. However one has only to sail close past the open entrance to see that it is unattractive to any kind of craft and harbours none. Not only is it very ancient and clogged with mud, but it offers none of the amenities of Ardglass which is hard by. At one time it was considered for rebuilding, but Kilkeel was chosen instead.

## Ardglass

See Chart No 44; there is a rather small plan in Chart No 633 which gives an unflattering impression of the place. The great mistake to avoid is to blunder into Killough Harbour which is only a mile to the south. Admitted, Ardglass S Pier needs an extension but it is a snug little place for all that. The approach is open and hazard-free, though for some reason there is often rough water here. There are two lights, the inner being sectored; the white light gives a true lead in. The beacon on the starboard hand rocks should be noted. The stone pier is tall and should be rounded slowly, on one occasion I came on a dredger sitting like a spider in the middle of the harbour surrounded by a web of warps. There are deep water berths inside the wall and along the quay, or an anchor can be dropped near the beacon on Churn Rock. Ardglass is a fairly busy trawler harbour, with boats dropping in during the day and homing at night and particularly at the week-end, so that one has to be prepared to shift berth as required. A shelving sand beach at the top can be used for catamarans.

The harbour is open to easterly weather which drives in a circular scend, making things uncomfortable at times. When this threatens or occurs, a boat can move to the N Pier in the old harbour leaving the two beacons to port. It is feasible to berth at the north pier and dry out with good shelter and not too much restriction on moving out. For absolute shelter there is the dock at the end of the pier which, though silted, has enough water for a yacht. This is aptly named God's Pocket and, being quayed all round, one can rig a gang plank and temporarily or permanently swallow the anchor. For some years an old salt water man, who held his Master's ticket in sail, lived aboard in God's Pocket.

The village is quiet and civilised without any detectable current of activism. It is possible to travel by bus to Belfast, though this would hardly rate as an attraction these days. It is best not to leave the boat unsupervised. Entry and Customs can be arranged by the Harbour Master.

## Strangford Lough

This entrance is even more challenging than that of Carlingford and neither it nor the Lough itself should be attempted without Chart No 2156 and the smaller scale No 1411, for two main reasons. First, the stream table shows a flow at springs of between seven and eight knots for most of the cycle, and secondly the Lough is strewn with rocks and pladdies. It resembles a large sponge, squeezed rhythmically by a giant hand with the intake and outflow using a long narrow neck. Frank

Cowper describes the flow (in his estimate, 10 knots) as 'the hottest tides in the United Kingdom and Ireland' except for the Swellies (through which he was swept in a gale) and the Pentland Firth. The difficulties if not the perils of the Strangford narrows are much elaborated in various pilots. They can however be quite safely overcome by ordinary cruising expertise and strict conformity with the tide tables and the wind at the entrance. It should be noted carefully that HW at Swan Island and in the Lough is two hours later than at Killard Point; which is not unexpected, for the distance to be covered is five miles and, as the entry wind is likely to be ahead, a strong and reliable engine is a necessity. The channel is not lit except for leading lights at Swan Island and Portaferry. Nor is it buoyed, but relies on a series of tracks and clearing lines the marks of which pass very quickly. These are charted and listed, as are the two sites of the Routen Wheel whirlpool each side of Rue Point. If the Wheel is actually seen, the passage has been wrongly timed.

The locating landmark is the large radar scanner on Killard Point with an initial course from Strangford fairway buoy to Butter Pladdy buoy, or using the Charted Track A. Some of the subsequent tracks are too long for easy identification except from a ship's lofty bridge. There is a considerable outflow on the ebb which, with strong winds, makes for a rough approach, but there is a beacon on St Patrick's Rock and, by keeping well up to Bar Pladdy, one should not make the mistake of using the west channel rather than the east. The essence of timing (bearing always in mind the two hours difference of HW at top and bottom) is to come up with the first of the flood, or at any rate wait till the hurry has gone out of the ebb. Slack water high is not to be trusted owing to the time difference and quick reversal of flow at springs. Exit may be a little safer at true HW slack, but is best left to the last of the ebb. There is no point whatever in trying to describe the entry passage, as every scrap of information is meticulously presented by the chart.

A proposal has been made that a barrage should be built across the narrows in order to generate electricity. The logistics of such a plan are probably sound, except that there is no present demand for the extra power. The Lough would be turned into a great boating lake, and it would probably mean that there would be no access for cruising boats, unless a passing lock were provided.

The logical place to pull out of the stream is at Strangford itself, where Swan Island gives sanctuary with some moorings but no anchorage room. Here the Harbour Master will help, provided there is no commercial traffic. The fairway of the car ferry has to be left clear and the full force of the stream can be seen as it crosses to Portaferry. The container traffic has now deserted the place and the village is once again quiet and peaceful. Just round Church Point there is good anchorage in or off Audley Roads, where one is out of the run, but for some antique reason a mooring fee is exacted. Portaferry is too scoured for a berth, but there are moorings and anchorage higher up in Ballyhenry Bay. Strangford village is an altogether charming place to stay, and Portaferry should be visited by car ferry to prove that no one is exaggerating the run of the tide.

The Lough proper is a miniature cruising ground in itself: an expanse of sheltered water twelve miles in length and two miles wide, justifying at least a week of intriguing exploration. Moreover there are several yacht clubs owing to its nearness to Belfast. Taking the port hand first, there is the Quoile YC at the navigable head of the River Quoile, and near its entry the Killyleagh YC. Heading back in the Lough again and using a charted bearing, there is Ringhaddy Sound which is not easy to find; here the water is deep and the moorings are laid by divers, but it is sheltered and offers the Ringhaddy YC. On the east side of the Lough there is Kirkcubbin Bay with anchorage and the YC. In addition there are numbers of bays and quiet anchorages. It should be understood that, though poles and perches on the pladdies are charted, there is no guarantee that they are still standing. The Strangford Lough YC at White Rock is the main club. Here there are many moorings, a hospitable clubhouse and a licensed bar.

### Portavogie

This harbour and its approaches are best shown on Chart No 2156. There is no harbour plan but the lay-out is clearly shown by my aerial photograph. The passage from Strangford Lough exit needs to be carefully studied on the chart, for there are clusters of drying rocks inside the South Rock light vessel, and a yacht should come well up to Plough Rock buoy and into the white sector of the Pier head light, before

*Portavogie.* Showing the thoughtfully designed basin with room for extension. *Author*

turning in. I have not visited the harbour in recent years, for the simple reason that until a new basin is added there is no room for yachts, particularly at week ends when all the trawlers are home; they are often packed so close that one could walk across the basin from side to side. Apart from Plough Rock there are no problems of entry.

The design of the harbour is admirable as it ensures that nothing comes in from an onshore gale, so that there is convincing all round shelter. The outer harbour has a spending beach and two piers. After the second wall there is a right-angled turn to starboard into the inner harbour. Ashore the village has all the usual supplies and a fish processing plant. The slogans have a markedly right wing loyalist slant and, coupled with this, the village is absolutely and determinedly dry. This cuts a yachtsman off from his main source of local gossip, but the reasoning behind it is good enough when one sees so much of the fisherman's hard-won money going over the bar counter in other ports. The nearest even mediocre pub is four long dusty miles away at Ballyhalbert to the north. There is no yachting presence or sailing club so that, unless things have markedly changed since I was last there, the harbour is best passed by except in emergency.

### Donagadhee

Chart No 1411 continues north to Lough Larne; chart No 3709 is essential. This chart, published in 1973, is in the 1980 edition and shows no IALA changes, possibly because none were required. The harbour could be an important staging

*Mew Island.* Showing the lighthouse and neighbouring radio mast which emits interfering signals. *Author*

*Donaghadee.* This aerial shot clearly shows that only the outer and most exposed part of the harbour is available for anchorage. *Author*

post for cruising yachtsmen though it is not well sheltered, accepting as it does everything from the north-easterly direction. The approach from the south is open enough: from Portpatrick the Copeland islands are left to the north. Mew Island has a particularly troublesome RDF frequency which obtrudes over most of the North Irish Sea. Though the crossing from Portpatrick is short, it must be remembered that the North Channel here should be tackled in good weather as it can be extremely rough and dangerous. Doneghadee Sound attracts a charted note of dangers to under-powered ships, though it is buoyed and the stream tables do not show rates above three knots. The Sound is otherwise the obvious link with Belfast Lough.

The harbour was built as a railway terminal for the short Portpatrick crossing, but was hardly used because of the crossing hazards. What it leaves for the yachtsman is more apparent than real. The harbour should be given a fairly wide approach as the Wet Scotchman Rock now has no perch, and the red sector of the pierhead light seems much narrower than it should be. The traditional method of berthing is to drop an anchor astern and nose into the South Pier; with any wind entering the harbour this is hardly a laughing matter. There are now moorings stretching across the harbour which are rather exposed, while there is room to anchor further out. The harbour dries inshore of the moorings. The town is well furnished and supplied and there is no shortage of pubs, in marked contrast to the picture at Portavogie.

31

**Belfast Lough**

This lough is fully charted in Chart No 1753, with the more distant approaches in Chart No 2198; the near approach by Donaghadee Sound is detailed in Chart No 3709. Yachtsmen might well expect that a large town and port would offer shelter independant of the political situation, which in itself is a powerful deterrent. However, as in the case at Liverpool, the dock system is for big ships and yachts will not be welcome except in stress of weather. Moreover, the rest of the large Lough has little convincing shelter and local owners are more inclined to use Strangford or Larne. The topography shows an open aspect from the east and NE, with pretty well equal access from the westerly direction. In the absence of any good harbour, settled weather is needed for exploration.

*Ballyhome Bay*
See inset plan in Chart No 1753. This is a wide shallow bay which is fully open to the north giving good southerly shelter and some westerly cover. The moorings of the Royal Ulster YC and the Ballyholme YC are charted and offer visitors' moorings and hospitality. Living aboard may be uncomfortable but there are slips and services. There is charted anchorage offshore.

*Bangor Bay*
See inset plan in Chart No 1753. As with Ballyhome Bay, the exposure is much the same but the bay is deepened with three solid piers, north, central and south, giving additional shelter from the north, see aerial photograph. It is significant that the North Pier is now in the process of extension, which may well improve the yacht shelter significantly. This extension may eventually lead to a good basis for a marina, but plans are held up for lack of money. There is certainly an urgent need for such a

*Bangor.* The main harbour, which is empty in this shot, lies between several piers to the right. Centrally is the Long Hole, with reasonable but limited shelter. *Author*

development in the Lough. The photograph also shows the primitive hurricane harbour of Long Hole. Access is over a sill with a depth inside of five feet; it is likely to be crowded but enquiries can be made for a berth. Given further protection it seems probable that Bangor could become the main yachting centre for the Lough.

## Cultra
Lying six miles further up in the Lough from Bangor are the charted moorings of the Royal Northern Ireland YC which, though still fairly exposed, gain rather better cover by being further inland. Visitors will find hospitality, slips and services here.

## Belfast Docks
Detail is laid down in the plan in Chart No 1753. The dredged channel is clearly marked though, once inside, the topography is going to prove puzzling. Small boats are accepted into the Spencer Dock. Belfast itself will not be attractive to visitors in the present emergency.

## Carrickfergus
There is no harbour plan, but details can be made out from Chart No 1753. This is well sheltered, with entry from the south, but it dries out completely to mud and is suitable only for boats that can take the ground at the walls; consequently there is little commercial or trawler activity. It has now been agreed in principle that a marina should be built here, though no details or timing are available at the time of writing. To the east of Carrickfergus there are the Kilroot power station harbour and the oil jetty at Cloghan Point.

### Lough Larne
The essential and fully detailed chart is that of No 1237; the approaches are covered by Chart No 2198. Larne is fifteen miles from Belfast by land and twenty miles by sea. The sea passage skirts the low-lying and undistinguished Island Magee, with the only hazard the romantically named Island of Muck. This island is unlit with just beyond it a sewer buoy. This is a weather shore with a lazy tide and a slack stream running along the coast on a north/south axis. North of Island Magee lie the Hunter Rock buoys with clear passage inside. Further north still lie the Maidens, a dangerous rocky complex which is lit, but again the passage to Loch Ryan lies well clear of them. Entrance to the Lough is well marked from the fairway buoy and well lit by sectored lights. Having however rounded Barr Point a yacht need not follow the deep channel, but can come closer in round Ferris point and out of the big ship traffic.

Once inside, it is best for a yacht to follow the left-hand bank, with careful chart reading of the off-lying man-made artifacts. Here there are two berthing possibilities. First the Boat Harbour, this is unfortunately just off the aerial picture, though the sewer outfall mark can be seen. There should be a berth here though no doubt crowded; it is however rather isolated and communication is by the nearby

*Larne.* The moorings can just be seen to either side of the peninsula. *Author*

ferry slip. A little higher up is the deep water tanker jetty with the power station on shore. There are charted boat moorings behind the jetty with a smaller slip ashore; these are liable to be fouled by oil spills. Secondly, having passed the power stations, there is a charted anchorage at Yellowstone which is well sheltered but rather remote.

One authority quotes the stream at the entrance as running up to 3½ knots and this may well be, since the Lough is a large inland lagoon, but nothing approaching this figure is noted in the stream chart. Initially the town side of the harbour is taken up by commercial services which have nothing to offer the yachtsman. However, beyond Phoenix Quay and all round Curran Point, there are well-sheltered moorings based on two yacht clubs with visitors' moorings; anchorage here is inadvisable. Further on there is even better shelter with a slip inside Curran Point. There are good services, but the town centre is a bus ride away with a good deal of anti-terrorist activity. In all then, Larne offers a good safe harbour as a staging post, before crossing to the Scottish side on the course of the Larne to Stranraer ferries.

# V   The Scottish Sector

**Charts**

| No | Title | Scale 1: |
|---|---|---|
| 1344 | Kircudbright bay. | 15,000 |
| 1346 | Solway Firth and approaches. | 100,000 |
| | Whitehaven harbour. | 7,500 |
| | Workington harbour. | 10,000 |
| 1403 | Loch Ryan; | 25,000 |
| | Stranraer harbour. | 10,000 |
| 1826 | Irish Sea – eastern part. | 200,000 |
| 2094 | Kircudbright to Mull of Galloway and Isle of Man. | 100,000 |
| 2198 | North channel – southern part. | 75,000 |
| Book | *Solway Sailing Directions and Anchorages* (See bibliography) | |

**The Crossing**

The crossing from Ireland to Scotland is covered by Chart No 2198. Of the two usual crossings of the North Channel, that between Donaghadee and Portpatrick is much the shorter: about 18 miles as compared with 33 from Larne to Stranraer. The former has, however, a bad reputation and many yachts have reported bad conditions with sudden changes when wind shifts against tide. It was abandoned as a ferry for sailing ships and in 1953 the car ferry *Princess Victoria* was overwhelmed. Unless one deliberately sets out for a tussle with the elements, it is suitable only for a quick dash in good weather. The stream rate table does not show high rates, but they may not be representative of the whole area. Slightly further north, the Larne–Stranraer car ferry route offers easier entry and better shelter at either end.

En route, the Hunter Rock and the Maidens (see photographs) are left to the north, while the Corswell light is ahead. There is no handy RDF beacon ahead on the Galloway coast; the nearby beacon on Mew Island is, however, loud and gives good back bearings. It should be noted that Corswell Point is not the mark for entry to Loch Ryan, the fairway buoy being three miles further north. My experience is that the Loch Ryan entry can be a teasing crossroads for yachts bound to and from Scotland, since there is often a lot of ferry traffic entering or leaving at full flank speed. As an alternative to entering Loch Ryan, the crossing can be planned direct to Portpatrick, providing always that there is no strong onshore wind, which would make entry difficult.

*West Maiden*. Looking very deserted, with an unpainted disused light. The sister rock is the site of the present lighthouse. *Author*

*East Maiden*. To the north of Larne. *Author*

*Corewell Point.* The lighthouse at the entrance to Loch Ryan. *Author*

## Loch Ryan

In addition to the approaches chart (No 2198), Chart No 1403 gives full details and a harbour plan. The axis of the Loch lies SE/NW so that gales, particularly from the prevalent NW, will enter freely. There is however a clear entrance and the good lighting allows entry by night, and at times when Portpatrick might be difficult. For immediate or temporary shelter, except from the NW, there are two anchorages a mile inside. There is shelter under the land from west and SW in Lady Bay, and from the north to east in Finnart's Bay. Use of either might save the trip to Stranraer.

Three miles in on the port hand is the lit Cairn Point, and anchoring is prohibited from there past the new ferry terminal. The foul ground marked inside the jetty was a World War II naval base now used for ship breaking, but it would need a good deal of cajolery to win a berth there. The Ro-Ro terminal is busy with ships sailing on time rather than tide. The important buoy lies a mile beyond Cairn Point, a green lit cone, warning visitors to keep outside the irregular spit off the Scar. Turning this, leads to the oddly named Wig which is the traditional yacht anchorage. Here there is shelter round to the NW, though swell comes in from the south. Ashore there are supplies from the caravan park shop and a small pub. The bay is however a convincing three and a half miles from Stranraer in isolated country. Moreover the surrounding hills are low, allowing winds to sweep down to make the harbour uneasy.

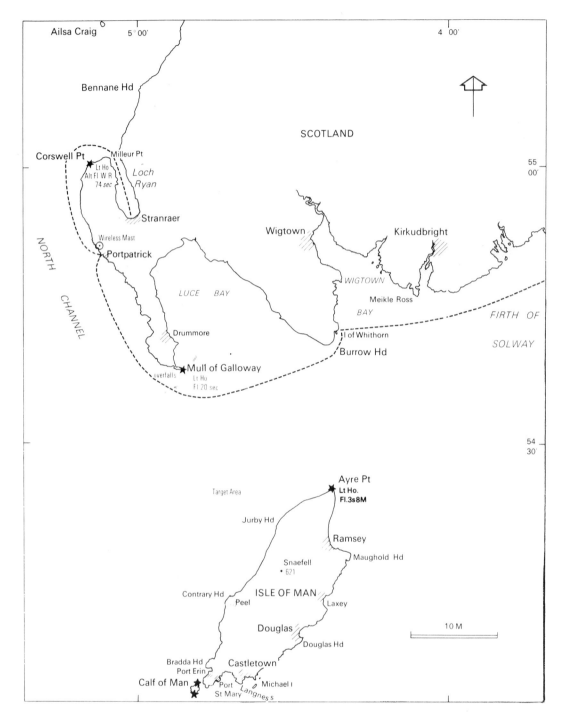

Fig. 4 Stranraer to Kircudbright. With the Isle of Man.

*Stranraer*

It should be noted that the Plan in Chart No 1403 included the effects of the dredging operations of 1979. The newer car ferry terminal includes the railway station making it a useful place for crew changes, though it is a tedious hundred miles from Carlisle. The older triangular harbour, being at the end of a long drift, has pretty well silted and no full attempt has been made to dredge it. The West Pier has however been much improved and there are berths alongside and approach by a dredged channel with port and starboard buoys. The Harbour Master reports six feet of water at LWST alongside in the inner harbour past the breakwater; the outer part of the West Pier which is outside the dredged channel has only two and a half feet. There is no anchoring in the west harbour and yachts should beware of the ferry turning area. The Harbour Master makes yachts very welcome and there are all facilities nearby. The yacht club is at the Wig.

The data shown for the West Pier in the plan in Chart No 1403 do not quite tally with a sketch plan drawn for me by the Harbour Master and dated 1981, in that on the chart the upper part is tinted green as drying; in reality the approach channel has a least depth of 1.4m (4 ft 6 in) with 1.5–1.8m (5–6 ft) depth beyond the breakwater knuckle. There is also anchorage off the shore to the west of West Pier, but naturally it would be best to go beyond the sewer beacon and keep close in, because of the prohibited anchorage line for the turning circle of the ferries.

In all however it can be seen that there has been a definite attempt to cater better for yachts here, though NW gales will still be disruptive.

## Portpatrick

The appropriate Chart is No 2198, but the only harbour plan is to be found in the Macmillan nautical almanac. The twenty-seven miles coast line of the Rhins of Galloway is a rather uninteresting stretch of the passage from the Irish Sea to Scottish waters. The stream runs strongly along the shore and a yacht can only go with the tide, while the narrowed North Channel often provides rough weather. From the south the usual course is via the Isle of Man and there are few harbours en route. Thus Portpatrick is a crucial staging port for cruising men, though it is a small place with a narrow entrance which is much impeded by onshore weather e.g. from the NW. From the north there is back-up from Stranraer, but it is necessary to avoid Craig Laggen which is quite unlit. The lighthouse on Black Head (Killantringan) is a mile and a half north of the harbour; a coaster was wrecked here only recently, immediately under the lighthouse. The harbour is clear from the west but obscured from the south and, though the radio masts pf Portpatrick radio stand out, there are other masts along the coast to the north.

By day the entrance is in clear view with water at all states for entry, but the crumbling harbour works are not reassuring. The main harbour lighthouse is disused and the green leading lights only visible from close in. In view of this poor lighting, the first-time visitor at night would probably opt for Stranraer. Inside the main dock the shelter is good, with only occasional swell getting in at HW.

*Portpatrick*. The ruinous entry with water at low tide. *Author*

*Portpatrick*. The deep-sided but fully enclosed basin. *Author*

As a matter of history, the harbour was started about a hundred and fifty years ago and eventually a rail spur and station was built to serve the short sea crossing to Northern Ireland. However the crossing was abandoned following some tragic losses of the sailing packets, and the longer but safer Stranraer to Larne passage adopted; many of the gravestones in the churchyard bear witness to the sad stories. The dock however was completed, though it never came into any real commercial use. In it, yachts are cramped and it can be a long drop to the deck after closing hours. The cruising atmosphere is good, though there is no sailing club; the waves break softly on the South Crescent and the little place drowses on with the occasional reek of peat smoke.

Though the dock is well enough kept up there is a clear need for improvement of entrance and lighting, before a yacht or the returning life boat misses the channel. At the moment the dock is owned or leased by a private company and the question of responsibility is not clear. The lighthouse needs to be reactivated and full power leading lights put in. It is surprising to find no radiobeacons along this coast.

### The Mull of Galloway
The relevant charts are Nos 2198 and 2094. The run south from Portpatrick is rather over fifteen miles, along an inhospitable lee shore. There is no shelter and even the small harbour at Port Logan is well exposed to the prevalent westerlies. At night the course would be laid on the light on Cramag Head. Coming from the south, the Mull of Galloway light should be left well to starboard and Cramag Head light again used. This gives a necessary clearance to the actual Mull, where the charted rips cover a large area when there is any strength in the wind. It is a matter of interested discussion as to whether the Mull of Kintyre or of Galloway gives the worse seas.

The stream runs hard north and south along the coast to Cramag Head and then switches though ninety degrees to fill and empty the Solway Firth, and pass mainly east of the Isle of Man into the Irish Sea; rates are tabulated up to four to five knots. If the Mull has to be rounded, it may be possible to pass close under the land and find a lee in East Tarbet Bay just inside the toe of the Mull. In crossing to and from the Isle of Man, this strong stream makes for a dicey landfall at either end. It is important to hit the Point of Ayre at the northern tip of the Island exactly, and luckily there is a radiobeacon here, and of course the lighthouse, though there are no beacons to the north. My ploy is to keep to the west and go into Peel, though this usually adds an extra day in going round south about. Moving north, there is a good point of departure from Ramsey and the Point of Ayre, and the Mull of Galloway should be identified early.

My own experience is that however the navigator makes his plans, he is likely to end up with a red face on this tricky crossing.

### The Solway Firth
As laid out in Chart No 1826, the chord of this bayed area stretches fifty miles from the Mull of Galloway to St Bee's Head in Cumbria, and penetrates to a depth of

forty miles. But as confirmed by the specific chart (No 1346) the area above the Maryport–Kippford line is uncharted. Only the coastline is mapped beyond this cruising limit, which lies waiting for the publication of a second *Riddle of the Sands*. For those sailing within the available ground, the guide *Solway Sailing Directions and Anchorages* is valuable for many of the following ports. The problems to be dealt with are shifting sands, tidal harbours, strong streams and poor shelter. For these reasons visitors fight shy of this cruising ground, though there is a good deal of local yachting activity and, given settled weather, a great deal to be seen on the Scottish side.

The approach from the Mull of Galloway has already been covered calling for a turning point, if possible, at low water slack. The more usual approaches are however from the south. Either from The Point of Ayre in the Isle of Man, or from Whitehaven, with landfall at the Isle of Whithorn or Kirkcudbright. The strong cross set in both passages has already been noted. Unfortunately the best radiobeacon is astern, at the Point of Ayre, but sometimes cross-bearings can be obtained on one of Mew Island, South Rock or Kintyre aerobeacon, all at extreme range.

*Luce Bay*
Chart No 2094 gives the largest scale. The use of this bay is largely precluded by an RAF bombing range, which leaves only southern parts of the shore open. The range is rarely used during the weekends, and warnings of its use are put out by radio and at Drumore. The range is ringed at the south end by six lit buoys, one of which lies two miles south of the unlit Scares, giving a useful warning of this nasty hazard.

There is cover in the lee of the Mull from the SW to NW. Just inside the toe, and out of the flood race, is East Tarbet Bay where one can wait for the tide, or take a welcome breath after struggling round. There is an anchorage well in, with a jetty near the road to the lighthouse but there are no other comforts. Three miles to the north is the civilisation of Drumore, which has been improved for the RAF range safety launch but can be entered by yachts; these can lie to the short quay and jetty, and take the ground. Otherwise there is fair westerly shelter by anchoring off between the harbour and the R and Y range buoy. There are supplies here and some yachting activity. Further up the coast there is charted anchorage in two small bays – New England and Chapel Rossan – the latter being the better. From here it is possible to walk three miles to the Tropical Gardens, which are probably the most northerly to flourish.

*Port William*
On the opposite side of the bay there is Port William which has anchorage somewhat exposed to the west; the harbour is small and dries. When the tide serves it can be entered and a berth found against the wall which will give reasonable shelter from the south. There are no charted lights at present, apart from the lit range buoy a mile out. The village has good supplies and services but no yacht club or Harbour Master, though there are berthing fees.

## The Isle of Whithorn

Chart No 2094 has the largest scale; there is a sketch plan of the harbour in *Solway Sailing Directions*. The approach leads round Burrow Head with entry two miles further on; the Head is without a lighthouse, but there is a red lit radio mast one mile inland. As can be seen from the chart, the stream runs up to four knots at springs, setting mainly to the west and putting up races round the Head; the stream also sets strongly across the harbour mouth. The entry is identified by the conspicuous square, white, St Ninian's Tower; the pierhead light has a four miles range. There is a rise of about fifteen feet at springs but the harbour dries. To seaward there is reasonably sheltered anchorage, but the entrance faces SE and from this quarter, in winter at least, heavy gales come in.

Entering after half flood it will be found that the pier has been rebuilt, with berths inside or along the quay. Enquiries for a mooring can be made to the Harbour Master or the Sailing Club. In the absence of S Easterly weather, this is an attractive harbour with reasonable services and a welcome for visitors. There is some trawler activity as well as yachting, and every help is given by the Wigtown Bay Sailing Club.

## Garlieston

See Chart No 2094 (there is no plan). This harbour lies five miles north of the Isle of Whithorn and has an open easy access, but the pierhead light is only occasional. There is fairweather anchorage off. It dries completely but is accessible after half flood, when it is possible to come in to berth at the pier or quay. This is in itself well sheltered but the entrance is fully open to the SE, and weather from this quarter will put in swell or worse. This means that one has to keep an eye on the forecast which might change during the time that the boat was dried out, making for a difficult decision as to whether it would be safe to stay when the water returned. With this proviso, it will be found that one can have a pleasant stay provided the wind stays in the right quarter.

## Wigtown Bay

See Chart No 2094. This is scarcely crusing ground, though there are a certain number of anchorages given suitable weather. These are fully covered in the *Solway Sailing Directions*. There are charted anchorages in the Islands of Fleet.

## Kirkcudbright

See Chart No 2094. The bay and harbour rates a special Chart (No 1344) which is crucial for the first timer. The *Solway Sailing Directions* provide detailed information, so that the cruising man has no excuse for not visiting. The top of the bay dries with a three mile well marked channel, while there is anchorage in the mouth to wait for water. The approach is open and located by Little Ross Island with the unmanned lighthouse (which has a twelve mile range). As can be seen from the chart, entry can be made by Little Ross sound, having noted Richardson's Rock at the entrance and Sugarloaf on exit – both unmarked. There is anchorage here near the jetty, providing the under water power cable is remembered. On the opposite shore there is temporary anchorage below Torrs Point, while the bar lies half a mile further in; entry is possible after half flood. The bay accepts everything from the south and particularly from the SE.

The channel at low water is merely the river bed across the sands of Dee, but it has 4½m (15 ft) of water on the top of the tide; there are numerous marks but they may vary from the charted characteristics. The stranger should be careful to leave early on the ebb. There will shortly be a harbour radio manned for two hours each side of high water to help the trawler fleet. At buoy No 21 the town reach is entered. It is best if yachts do not berth at the town quay because of trawlers, though these are not usually active at the week-end. The Harbour Master will probably direct one to the nearby wooden jetty where the boat should to be watched down, and perhaps needs pile barge boards. Moorings which are rarely vacant, dry to mud. In heavy up-country rain there are minor flash floods.

The town is a cheerful place, provided a comfortable berth can be fixed, and well supplied; it is completely sheltered.

## Hestan Island and Kippford

See Chart No 1346; there is a plan in the *Solway Sailing Directions* together with notes on the minor harbours, though on the whole these are rarely suitable for cruising boats. Kippford lies ten miles east of Kirkcudbright and is the main yachting centre in the Firth. On leaving Kirkcudbright a tank firing range lies to the east. If the red flag is flying, then it is necessary or advisable to keep five miles offshore round Abbey Head. Hestan Island, with its lighthouse and seven mile range light, marks the approach to Kippford. There is deep water anchorage either side of the island but the bay inshore has nothing to offer. As so frequent on this coast, the entry is open and faces SE, with obvious exposure – though the name of Rough Firth is derived from the island. The channel dries to the river bed, with Dalbeattie well up stream.

The channel starts well to the east, close to Castle Point and Craig Roan, but there is no fairway buoy; there are some locally laid buoys, though the banks may shift. It is necessary to come in on the flood and echo sounder and, though there is a sharp dog leg, there is no real difficulty in getting in. Eventually the moorings show straight ahead. Anchor off the jetty and enquire for a mooring, some at least of which do not dry.

As befits an active sailing centre, there is good shelter, a good clubhouse and a boatyard, as well as a welcome for visitors. Supplies and services are adequate for a long stay.

It remains to say that there is no possibility of cruising east of Kippford, and access to either Annan or Dumfries will need very good local knowledge or a professional pilot.

# VI   The Cumbrian Coast

## Charts

| No | Title | Scale 1: |
|----|-------|----------|
| 1346 | Solway Firth and approaches; | 100,000 |
| | Whitehaven harbour; | 7,500 |
| | Workington harbour. | 10,000 |
| 1826 | Irish Sea – eastern part. | 200,000 |
| 1961 | Rossal Point to St Bee's Head. | 75,000 |

### Solway Firth – South Coast

The most detailed chart is No 1346, but the area is also covered by No 1826. This is not a coast often visited by yachts but, since the south bank of the Solway is reserved for explorers, civilisation begins faintly at Silloth. The spring stream is still running between three to four knots here. The harbours were originally built for the iron ore trade both import and export, and the chart carries a note that the furnace fires may obscure the harbour lights – however this is a little outdated today. Only at Workington is there any commercial activity, and there is a constant battle against silting both from the sea and the rivers. The eastern coast of the Irish Sea is a lee shore and shelter is not good.

### Silloth

Chart No 1346 does not carry a harbour plan, so that detail has to be obtained from the magnifying glass. In the approaches however full charting, marking, and lighting is maintained. There is a harbour radio on the air round high water, and entry is free of hazard. The harbour dries, making entry on the flood necessary, but it is quayed round; it is sheltered except from heavy weather from the NW. There is a high rise and fall. The harbour is a base for a small inshore fishing fleet which works the banks for shrimp. A yacht is an unusual visitor, but reasonable supplies are to be had.

### Maryport

See Chart No 1364 (there is no harbour plan). The port was abandoned in 1953, but the pierhead light is still maintained, with a range of four miles. On the passage from Silloth there is a shifting bar which, in view of the stream, will be crossed on the ebb. There are three lit green conical buoys which give adequate guidance, so long as it is remembered that, due to the direction of buoyage, they must be left to port on entry. There are no approach hazards but entry is across drying sands.

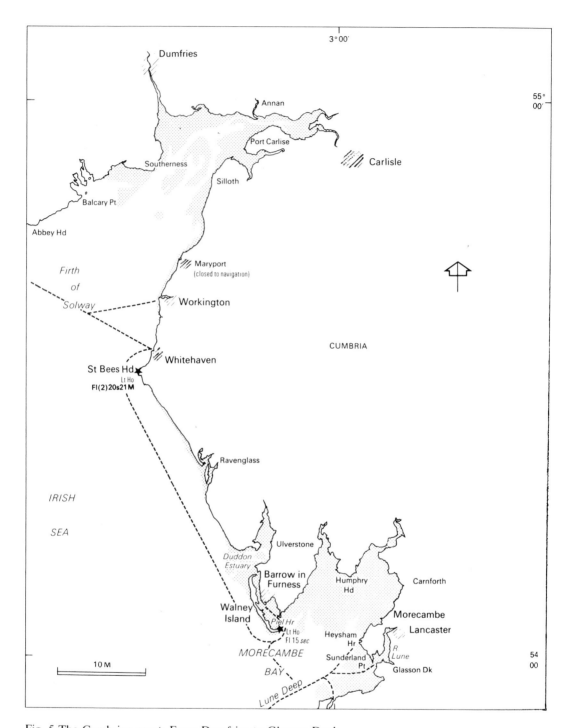

Fig. 5 The Cumbrian coast. From Dumfries to Glasson Dock.

When I last saw this harbour it was a scene of dreadful industrial decay. The dock gates had been left open and mountains of mud had accumulated from the River Ellen. The approach channel had been left undredged and a shingle bank was half across the entry. In more recent years Maryport has clawed back to some extent into the yachting picture. There is sailing club, and shallow draft boats can come in, though it would be unwise to try this in keel boats. There is complete shelter inside but it is not a place that a visitor would chose when running for shelter. There are full supplies in the town.

### Workington

In Chart No 1364 there is a harbour plan. Approach via English Channel (not *The English Channel*) is hazard-free with the North Workington buoy three miles offshore. The south pierhead light has a range of eight miles and, in addition, a complex of leading lights defines the channel exactly. This channel and the approach to the Prince of Wales dock has to be dredged constantly in view of the silt brought down by the River Derwent. There appears to be an error in the plan, important to yachtsmen in that the bridge cutting off the tidal harbour and the river is shown as

*Workington.* Dredging is constantly needed to keep the entrance open. *Author*

swinging. In fact it is now fixed, so that a fair amount of otherwise good shelter is lost to yachts, though used by cruisers, but with entry at all states, the harbour is a good refuge in heavy weather. Yachts cannot be entertained in the dock but might be allowed to berth temporarily at the north jetty dependent on dock traffic. A better initial bid would be to tie up to the outer wall of the dock near the life boat, when entering during the flood. With heavy weather from the NW there will be swell coming in, but from all other directions the cover will be good.

There remains the old Tidal Dock by the main pier, though this dries to deep mud. The moorings here are the province of the Vanguard SC; there are nineteen of these, all in full use, but it may be possible to use a vacancy. At the bottom of the tide it has to be foreseen that the boat will be cut off from the shore by mud. The town provides all supplies but, with the prevalent industrial decay, the harbour is very much short of charm; it would not tempt the visitor except for shelter.

### Harrington

There is no harbour plan on Chart No 1364. The entry lies three miles in from South Workington buoy, and the three miles range pierhead light is still maintained. It is open to the west, dries well out, but the piers give fair shelter from other directions. Previously a small coal and ore harbour, there is no commercial traffic now and only inshore fishing. It is possible to berth to the piers and dry out, but the only real yachting activity is seen when Irish races finish here.

### Whitehaven

Chart No 1364 carries a harbour plan. Lying three miles north of St Bee's Head, this feature locates it. Formerly the Head was the site of one of the oldest coal burning lighthouses, and coal has been won thereabouts for centuries. The place is easily located with a strong light on the West Pier.

Winds between west and north beat heavily on the Bar but there is a wide entry and no off-lying hazards. Protecting walls have been gradually built outwards and the inner harbour is fully sheltered. The charted drawback is that it dries to mud completely, being underlined to five metres at the top of the harbour. Several piers provide ample wall space, against which boats can be watched down to the deep soft mud. The Queen's Dock is not open to yachts but is used to off-load lighters from ships standing off. Visiting boats should make for the Old Quay rather than anywhere else. Moorings are laid in the south harbour by the local sailing club who have a clubhouse ashore. Since they dry out, however, they are of little use to a cruising boat. Trawlers mostly use the Custom House harbour, but their numbers have been much reduced following the cod wars.

All services are fully available together with supplies in the bustling town, while the SC offers hospitality. The whole of the Lake District is close inland. Apart from the limitation of having to sail on the tide, Whitehaven is an active yachting centre and very well sheltered, making it a very acceptable port of call when cruising.

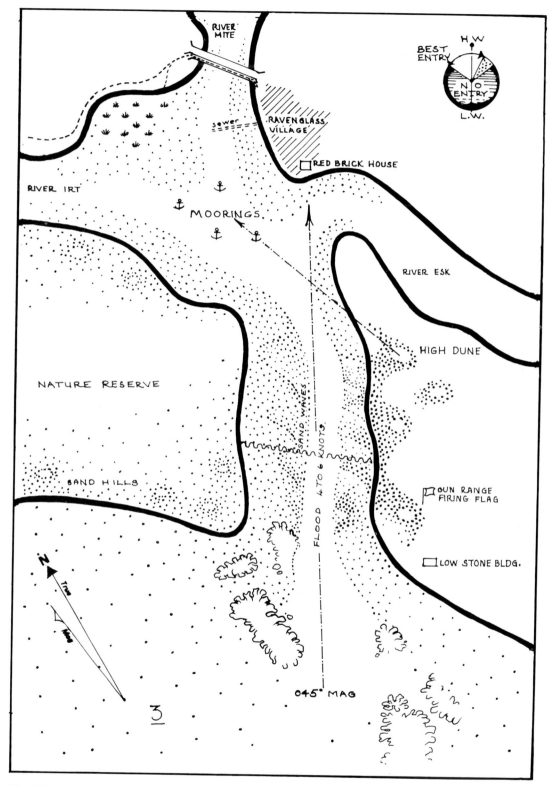

Fig. 6 Ravenglass.

**Ravenglass**

See Chart No 1346. There is no plan, but the local SC can provide in advance a useful sketch map, and maintains perches and buoys since there is no charting of the inlet. After rounding St Bee's Head and coasting southwards, the Calder Hall power station lies five miles north of the entry. The lit Selker buoy is three miles to the south and should be noted, so that passage is made outside it to avoid the Selker Rocks on the outward passage. For many miles to seaward the mark is the glacier smoothed dome of Black Combe, from which is carried the regular pounding of the Easkmeals proving ground.

Ravenglass dries out with a few pools. There is a sand bar offlying, so that westerly winds may prevent entry and visitors should only come in after four hours flood. There is a maximum flow of 4–6 knots at springs. With their kind permission, I have reproduced the Sailing Club's sketch map which is self explanatory. The shelter inside is good when taking into account the long period of drying out. It is an attractive place and well worth a visit for a boat that can take the ground to enjoy the remoteness; there are modest supplies, and the sailing club is most helpful.

*Duddon Mouth*

The best chart is No 1961. There is no official buoyage but some local perching of the channel. The two obvious difficulties are complete drying out and the very definite bar. The only point in going in is to visit Haverigg, some three miles inland from the bar. This is a remote but pleasant and a friendly place, with some yachting activity. A first entry would, however, call for local guidance.

# VII Morecambe Bay

## Charts

| No | Title | Scale 1: |
|----|-------|----------|
| 1826 | Irish Sea – eastern part. | 200,000 |
| 1961 | Rossal Point to St Bee's Head. | 75,000 |
| 1981 | Approaches to Preston. | 75,000 |
|  | Preston docks. | 10,000 |
| 2010 | Morecambe bay. | 37,500 |
|  | Fleetwood harbour. | 12,000 |
| Book | *Harbours in Morecambe Bay* (See bibliography) | |

## Morecambe Bay

Chart No 2010 covers the area specifically, with the approaches in Chart No 1826; Charts No 1961 and No 1981 are also relevant. The ten mile chord of the bay stretches as can be seen from the bastion of Walney Island in the north to the outcrop of Fleetwood in the south. Between these points the sea has made an inroad in the dunes twenty miles deep. The majority of this large drowned area is very shallow and dries to miles of sterile sand. Thus in crossing the bay it is as well to keep outside a line drawn from the cooling towers at Fleetwood and the castle on Piel Island. Even so, the echo sounder will show only a few feet of water, while the coast will be miles away over the sandy horizon; old harbours such as Ulverston, Grange and Arnside are now largely inaccessible. In the north there is limited access to the bay via the Barrow Channel.

In the south there is the remarkable phenomenon of the Lune deep, through which the bay largely drains. This is a steep-sided permanent underwater rift which stands between schemes for large scale reclamation of the area. When coming in from the north the echo sounder runs wild: from showing depths of a few feet, the needle rushes round the dial and starts on a second trace to finish up showing depths of over a hundred feet. Inshore it continues like the bed of a river, reaching Fleetwood, the Lune and Heysham, until it peters out at Morecambe. Yachtsmen have to learn not to take short cuts, for there are no marks across the sands which form the majority of the bay. The main entry to the bay is focused on the Morecambe Bay light buoy; this has replaced the lightship and is an intense high focal plane light at the tip of Shell flat. Eight miles further in is the Lune Deep buoy; it acts as the fairway buoy. Thereafter the channel is buoyed and the whole entry is an interesting night exercise in picking up and counting the IALA flashes and finding the greens.

*Walney Island.* The lighthouse is on the southern tip. *Author*

### The Morecambe Bay Gas Field

Ten miles further out from the Morecambe Bay buoy, the oil field is not yet exactly charted and shows as yet only one well, which I assume is the initial tap. Within a few years, however, this will be in active operation and of great significance to yachts using Morecambe Bay. I understand that six taps are planned and that these will use a pipe line to the shore, landing at the north end of the bay beyond Barrow. Some time back, an efficient pipe-laying barge lying off Heysham completed the shore-link in short time (it could lay a mile of pipe per day) so it looks as if the scheme will be functioning without delay and will set up an intriguing new hazard in the Irish Sea. It is worth noting the radiobeacons on the coast at Walney Island and Blackpool airfield.

52

There is a good deal of yachting activity in the accessible parts of Morecambe Bay, and quite a handful of sailing clubs. But to be objective, this is more a matter of the local inhabitants struggling against poor conditions rather than enjoying the beauties and benefits of the area. Apart from large stretches of sand and mud, the bay is fully open and offers a lee shore from the wide west; Fleetwood is being encroached upon; the one purpose-built harbour at Heysham is closed to yachts; and the excellent marina at Glasson Dock is tidal in approach.

**The Barrow Channel**

The key chart is No 3164, the inshore detail not being charted in Nos 2010 and 1961. Chart No 3164 shows a complex topography. Walney Island is like a coral reef of elongated eccentricity sheltering a muddy lagoon, the northern end of which is lost in the waste of Duddon Sands and barred by the fixed bridge at Barrow. At the southern end, the toe of Walney together with the islands of Piel, Roa, and Foulney form the old Piel (not Peel) harbour. In the past this gave rather vague shelter to the ships of the iron ore trade, and was probably a perquisite of Cockersand Abbey, regulated from Piel Castle; the row of pilot's cottages, with their telescope windows,

*Piel Harbour.* Looking SW over Foulney, Roa, Piel and Walney Islands. *Author*

is still extant on Piel. From offshore the marks are Walney Lighthouse (radiobeacon FN) and the castle ruins.

The big ship fairway buoy is well out at Lightning Knoll, but yachts may break into the channel between the outer and inner Bar buoys; there is water at all times and no real bar because of dredging. Round LW, however, I have found it embarassingly easy to run on at the narrows at the green can buoy on Haws Point East. Conversely there is a high rise and I have seen a new 200,000-ton bulk carrier come out in a gale. Close attention is needed to the buoyage and more still to the series of lit leading marks, the key leg being Beacons Nos 3 and 4.

*Piel Island*

Chart No 3164; see also my aerial photographs. The anchorage lies roughly inside the three buoys – Scar, Piel and Ridge just out of the channel – though its traffic is sparse. The Piel buoy marks a bank on which one might dry out unexpectedly, a visitor's trap. There are also a number of moorings, many of which are suspect, and much old chain on the bottom. The shingle beach takes catamarans, and there is a good stone slip. The stream runs strongly off the beach, causing difficulty in getting back aboard on dark nights. During the week the place is deserted but at weekends there may be a ferry service, in addition to which many weekend cruisers come in. The focus of attraction is the old pub at the top of the slip, with elastic opening hours. Other than liquid there are no supplies on the island, and these have to be obtained on Roa island.

As can be seen from the chart, the shelter in Piel Harbour is by no means full, but it usually suffices through weather that would prevent one from going outside. In any case it is always possible to beat a retreat up to Barrow. It cannot be said that Piel Harbour offers much charm in itself, though there is nostalgia in its long story. It is a rallying place for all the Morecambe Bay clubs, where one can meet other minor adventurers and roister and yarn about the Irish Sea.

*Piel Island.* Showing moorings off the Pilots' cottages. *Author*

54

Labels on image: Causeway → to Foulney I; SC jetty; Public jetty; Barrow Channel

*Roa Island.* Looking NE towards the causeway to Foulney Island from the mainland; the moorings dry out. There is deep water this side of the island, between the sailing club jetty and the public jetty. The Foulney causeway runs off the main causeway to Roa Island. *Author*

### Roa Island

See Chart No 3164. Crossing the narrow Piel channel we are in civilisation again with telephone, Post Office, buses and so on. There is less room out of the channel for moorings than at Piel, and these may have to be sought above Head Scar; those to the west of the island are for shallow draft boats only. The embankment running to the mainland carries an old railway as well as the road and was no doubt used for the ore trade; a similar embankment, now disused, ran out to Foulney Island. As well as the public jetty, the Roa Island SC have their own jetty and clubhouse.

### Barrow

See Chart No 3164 with plan. It is hardly likely that sailing men would want to cruise to the harbour for its charm or their own pleasure, for there is no great yachting presence, even though there is a sailing club; the main preoccupation is sea angling. Once decided, however, the passage is well buoyed and at the top there is good shelter. The bridge is charted as lifting, but this is unlikely for yachts, and

*Barrow.* Looking east; anchorage and moorings are north of the building slip to the left. *Author*

indeed it is scheduled to become fixed. The gantries of the shipyard are a landmark well out to sea. Ramsden Dock may accept yachts but, in the main, the large system is unused except for some Ro-Ro traffic, as can be seen from the photograph. Since there should be at least half-tide entry, this is another dock that would make a good yacht marina; there are plenty of potential customers, now exposed in Piel Harbour, to use it conveniently and safely. But as usual, sailing men do not seem to think in terms of marinas in the NW. At least above No 22 buoy there is anchorage and, higher up still, some moorings. The great advantage is that full shelter is assured here.

Having now covered the Furness end of the Bay, the depths of the rest of the area are only safely accessible by striking across into the Lune deep. In this passage over the banks I feel happier in keeping well to the west and using Fleetwood cooling towers as a forward mark. Bolder spirits will cut across to Heysham power station, or even Morecambe, but there are no marks out in the bay, and the low readings on the echo sounder deter me from going too far east.

*Fleetwood.* Looking south at low water. The commercial port is to the right, with the yacht club moorings at Knott End to the left. *Author*

## Fleetwood

Refer to Chart No 2010 with harbour plan; Chart No 1961 covers the more distant approaches. The Lune Deep buoy marks entry to the Lune Deep; the Wyre channel fairway buoy lies six miles further ahead. Since the Lune fairway buoy is only one and half miles further in, there is a possibility of confusion. The cooling towers of the Fleetwood power station make a good landmark. The old Wyre lighthouse is now out of position and disused. As can be seen, the channel is well marked with water at all states. It has recently been deepened so that the Ro-Ro ferries can sail to a timetable, and these may be met in the channel – outward in the morning and back at night. The trawler fleet on the other hand, is more closely tied to HW to enter and leave the Fish Dock. Recent dredging has rather restricted the mooring area and the tackle tends to be sanded down; for this reason the moorings previously maintained by the Blackpool and Fleetwood YC have been given up. It is best to pick up a vacant mooring on arrival rather than anchor; then, using the slip of the Knott End SC (which extends to low water), come ashore and speak to the boatman who is very helpful.

Though on paper the harbour is exposed to the north, the shelter offered is very real, particularly round to the NW. In practice the off-lying sands dry early and do not allow much weather in, except in the combination of springs, a northerly gale and surge. There are supplies in Knott End village, whence the ferry runs to Fleetwood. It cannot be said that the prospect at low water is in any way attractive, but the people in this part are good-hearted and the bonus is that Fleetwood is one of the safest places hereabouts to sit out a gale.

*Skippool Creek*

The River Wyre is uncharted above Fleetwood, but it is navigable on the tide for about another four miles to the Shard toll bridge. Though unbuoyed, the passage is straightforward in the middle of the river, and described in the Morecambe Bay pilotage book which is noted at the start of this section and is published by the Blackpool and Fleetwood YC. Their headquarters is at the top of the reach on the starboard hand, with boats lying to stages in the creek; there is a good slip and clubhouse and visitors can be accommodated. It is not advisable to anchor off because, when the tide goes away, the boat will be surrounded by the blackest mud imaginable. On the opposite bank half way up is Wardleys creek, where both the Wyre and the Wardleys SC's have their moorings. In both places there is excellent shelter.

**The River Lune and Glasson Dock**

Chart No 2010 is still relevant though it only gives the topography and omits the buoyage; there is not much further help in the Macmillan and Reed's almanacs. The navigation of the Lune has always been an intriguing challenge as an approach to the old port of Lancaster; this has long ceased to be a port, but the commissioners are still the authority controlling the river. Glasson Dock was completed in 1787 and is still working commercially, being used by ships drawing twelve to fifteen feet. The extensive canal basin (vintage ca 1830) opens off the sea dock and is currently the site of the only marina in the Irish Sea. This, combined with the complete shelter offered by both basins, makes Glasson important from the yachting angle.

Being such a period piece of maritime archaeology, the sea dock does not boast an entry lock. With the result that the gates only open for a brief hour or so before tidal high water. From April to October they open for each HW (but in the winter only for daylight HW). Closure can be delayed for a while but once shut they cannot reopen, so that arriving before they close on the start of the ebb is the basis of the navigational plan. For late arrivals, it is possible to dry out alongside up-river, facing the outer wall, where ship-breaking is carried out.

As can be seen from the chart, the approach to the River Lune is straightforward enough. From the Lune Deep buoy it is five miles to Fleetwood No 1, and thereafter another one and a half miles to the Lune No 1 buoy; all three buoys are IALA shaped and lighted. In the current chart it is disconcerting to find that, though the river is noted as buoyed to Glasson Dock, no buoys are shown on the chart. The

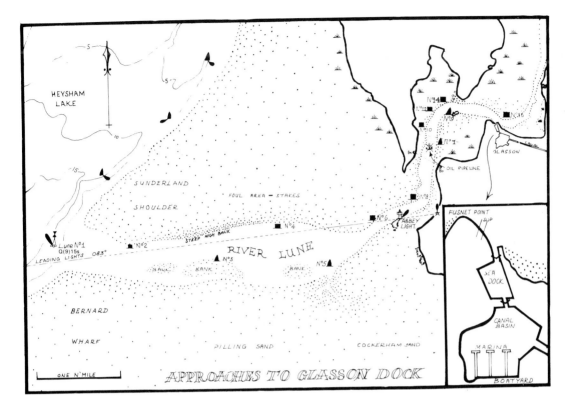

Fig. 7 Glasson Dock.

omission is supposedly due to shifting of the banks, but it is probably more likely to be due to the buoys themselves not being up to Trinity House standards. Under the new Harbour Master at Glasson these have now been brought up to scratch and put into service. It is anticipated that a new chart covering Fleetwood, the Lune and Heysham will be published within a year or two, meanwhile a sketch map is reproduced here. Within the river there is a series of training walls, seen on aerial photography, but they will not impede yachts until one hour after HW. The port radio link (VHF 16 & 19) operates two hours before HW.

The tides in the Lune do not conform to the usual pattern. Thus one will look in vain for the predicted HW at Glasson Dock in the tide tables; the LW predicted time at the Lune No 1 buoy is the same as for Fleetwood. Glasson is however 2½–3m (8–10 ft) above chart datum for Morecambe Bay and six miles distant, with the result that the flood does not reach here until three hours after LW Fleetwood. In effect the flood runs only for three hours at Glasson (two hours at Lancaster), and ebbs for nine hours. The dock gates can only open when inside and outside levels balance, and they close soon after the ebb starts, giving a period of about an hour. The Harbour Master can extend this only for commercial traffic.

With this deadline for arrival, the exercise revolves round the time limits between

*Glasson Dock.* There is a lock between the sea dock and the marina in the freshwater basin. *Author*

which one can depart from the fairway buoy; these limits are fairly narrow and depend on how long it will take the yacht to cover the distance. In this regard it will need to be remembered that the spring flood will run up to four knots. Locally it is considered best to start about 2 hours after low water which gives time in hand for anchoring off and waiting for the gates. If the start is delayed till four hours after LW, then there is still perhaps a sporting chance; within the next two hours there may be a chance to get up to Glasson and stay outside the dock. Later than this it may be possible to get as far as Abbey Hole at the lighthouse and perhaps stay afloat at anchor if the weather is settled. Beyond Sunderland Point there is an oil pipeline and anchoring is prohibited; if it does not seem wise to stay either at the Abbey Hole or at Lune No 1, then Fleetwood can be entered at any state of the tide.

My aerial photograph shows the overall layout of Glasson Dock. First the sea dock, with the connecting lock to the large area of the freshwater canal basin leading into the Lancaster Canal. The lock, the berths on the north side and the canal are operated by British Waterways. The two hundred berth marina (currently the only marina in the Irish Sea) is owned by the Glasson Basin Yacht Company. On entering the sea dock, short stay boats can remain there under the direction of the Harbour Master. There is complete shelter but a fair amount of commercial activity.

It has to be admitted that using the marina staging berths, as I do, takes all the fun out of Irish Sea cruising. There is no exposure to gales, no mud larking, no dinghy work, no rise and fall and no warp tending; barnacles do not thrive in the fresh water. Having accepted these blessings, Glasson remains antiquely unspoiled and still accepts coasters with up to twelve feet draught, though of limited beam, quite actively; it is only six miles from the motorway, though the branch railway line is now closed. The Lancaster Canal has forty-two miles of contour waterway without locks, though blind at both ends. Five miles further up the Lune is Lancaster, where it is possible to dry out alongside the old warehouses in the centre of the town. After a long uphill fight, the tide just reaches the city but is very soon away.

*Heysham*. The big building is a nuclear power station, with cooling water intake. *Author*

**Heysham**

The definitive chart is No 1552 but No 2010 is also needed. The harbour lies four miles NE of Lune No 1 buoy and is approached by a well-buoyed channel through Heysham Lake. It is dominated by the nuclear power station (cooling water intake in the approach) and the first phase is about to go on stream. It is a purpose-built railway dock nearly half a mile long, fully dredged with entry at all states; the entry accepts some swell from the NW. Owned by Sealink it is a commercial dock but, as the photograph shows, there is plenty of unused quay space. In the context of Morecambe this sounds wonderful to a yachtsman, but alas yachts are not allowed to use it except under stress of weather, so that the whole of this well-sheltered base is denied to them. By the simple provision of pontoons, a profitable marina could be made within the dock, and one has only to look at the traditional exposure at Morecambe two miles away to see numerous potential clients. There are daily Ro-Ro services from Heysham and it seems likely that this harbour will be the servicing base for the Morecambe Gas Field.

**Morecambe**

Chart No 2010 continues in use, there is no plan and there is no official buoyage north of Heysham. The visitor is thus left to wander among the shoaling Morecambe Bay sandbanks, so that he must have a minimum of clear weather and a suitable state of tide. There is a spring rise of about 8 metres (27 feet) but a quick run off, so that by half ebb most of the anchorage has dried to mud. With a draft of less than 1¼m (4 feet), yachts may still float between the Stone Jetty and the Central Pier but only at neaps and at the risk of an uncomfortable berth. The local boats moor beyond the Town Hall slipway, drying out at half ebb with a walk ashore across the mud. There is no question of any harbour shelter and the shore is quite open from west to north. With these few advantages there is a surprising amount of yachting activity and a keen sailing spirit. However this is against a full background of local knowledge which a visitor is unlikely to possess. The same applies regarding access to Arnside above Morecambe, which is now sanding further with result that even at the right state of tide the water is likely to run out before the approach is completed. In addition, fishing stakes have now become a local hazard between Heysham and Morecambe.

**Charts**

| No | Title | Scale 1: |
|---|---|---|
| 1826 | Irish Sea – eastern part. | 200,000 |
| 2094 | Kircudbright to Mull of Galloway and I of Man. | 100,000 |
| 2696 | Plans in the Isle of Man: | — |
| | Douglas Bay. | 7,500 |
| | Ramsey Bay; Calf Sound; Peel; Port Erin. | 10,000 |
| | Castletown Bay; Bay Ny Carrickey. | 20,000 |
| Book | *Cruising Guide to the Isle of Man* (See bibliography) | |

Sited in the middle of the northern half of the Irish Sea, the Island has sailing links with all the surrounding coasts, and it is a favourite rendezvous for the Morecambe Bay boats. It is a miniature cruising ground in itself, especially if a circumnavigation is planned to savour the west coast as well as the east. I have been able to go into much greater depth and detail in my separate book *Cruising Guide to the Isle of Man*, and readers anxious for more information should look to the bibliography.

*Navigation*

In the approaches there are marine radiobeacons at Creigneish (for Port St Mary), Douglas, and the Point of Ayre (a geographical location not to be confused with the Point of Air or Ayr in NE Wales); each of these has a range of fifty miles, and there is a limited range aerobeacon at Ronaldsway airport. Sudden sea mists are a speciality of the island coasts; known as Mannin mists, they are said to be organised by the old god Manamanin from his seat near Kirkmichael. He reasoned that the only way to deal with the many invasions of the past was to shroud the shores of the island in fog; this he still disconcertingly continues to do when yachts approach.

The tidal pattern is based on the picture of the north-going and the south-going flood streams meeting round the island, the tidesmeets being at Contrary Head on the west coast and at Maughold Head to the east. On the west coast and over towards Ireland there are very weak streams, but on the east side there are spring streams running up to five knots from the Calf going northward. Though they are purely coastal they play havoc with a clean entry to Douglas, for instance. The strong east-west stream to the north of the island causes equal trouble with landfalls in both directions. Strong winds make the rounding of either end of the island

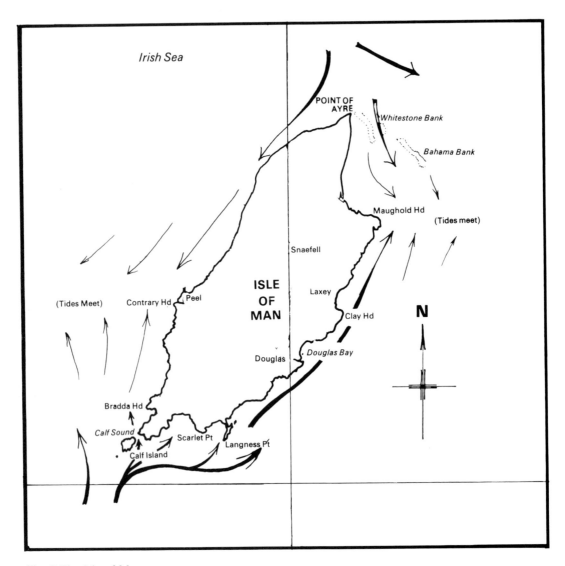

Fig. 8 The Isle of Man.

tricky, and the Point of Ayre can be quite nasty on the wrong timing. A detailed analysis of the round the island streams can be obtained from the Manx SC at Ramsey.

The rise and fall is usually more than twenty feet and HW is within a few minutes of Liverpool and Dover at all the harbours. Deep keel boats are at a discount here, for there are few places where they can lie afloat without being exposed from one or more quarters. In contrast, drying out alongside in the inner harbours gives comfort and full shelter even if tidebound.

*Facilities*

The high holiday season is short, mainly July and August. Outside these times in May, June and September the island is not overcrowded. There is busy trawler traffic in the herring season in the autumn, and people crowd into the island for the TT races. Most of the commercial traffic and the Ro-Ro ferries use Douglas where harbour works to improve the shelter are now going forward.

Many of the internal services of the Isle of Man are now autonomous: customs, currency, postage and telephones among others; the harbours are under one authority, and dues for one week can be paid at any of the harbours. The main port of entry is Douglas but yachts are accepted at any harbour – form C 1328 should be filled; passports are not yet required. Though there is an air service, most supplies and visitors came by sea. To hire a car, driving and insurance certificates are needed.

To my mind the attraction of the island from the yachtsman's point of view is the gentle nostalgia, fixed about the beginning of the century when the herring were harvested by the local sailing fleets. Almost nothing has been done to alter or spoil the harbours since then, or to foresee the advent of yachting. Outside Douglas, and particularly in the off season, one can pick up the reek of peat smoke and be back in an era of invasions and smuggling. There is of course no question of any marina or indeed no really suitable site for one; as all the inner harbours are tidal, a lock would be needed, with limited time of access.

**Douglas**

See overall Chart No 2094 and Plan in Chart No 2696. The distant approaches are made clear by the high ground of the island, and by night there is the distinctive six flash light on Douglas Head. The RDF beacon (DG) is located on Victoria Pier but the symbol does not appear in Chart No 2695, though it is shown in Chart No 2094. The lighthouse has no fog signal, this is also on Victoria Pier, but only as a high pitched whistle; the bell on the Battery Pier is ineffectual. Conister Rock or Isle of Refuge lies close north of the entry. These close approach points are important for, though the entry is open, my experience is that in summer the Mannin mist is fairly common. The lay-out is well shown in the aerial photograph. Beware of ferries, which come out stern first and then turn.

The harbour has hitherto been fatally open from NE to SE, which can make the outer harbour untenable in gales and in recent years wrecked the Ro-Ro berth; as a result, an improvement scheme is currently being carried out for completion in 1983. Among other things there is to be a 500 yd lengthening of the breakwater, which at least will cover the SE exposure.

Visting yachts must report to the Harbour Master at the end of the King Edward Pier. Anchoring in the outer harbour is not allowed, and use of the few moorings is not encouraged; there are three possibilities for berthing. In the Croak there are now three large mooring buoys to which yachts tie up like the spokes of a wheel. This is done by dropping an anchor astern and putting a warp onto the buoy or vice

*Douglas Head.* Above the lighthouse is to be seen the Camera Obscura. *Author*

*Douglas.* Victoria pier is on the right of the inner harbour, while King Edward VIII pier is left; this dries to half way. *Author*

versa; which can be quite a feat of seamanship if there is wind entering the harbour. The berth is comfortable enough in the right conditions but it should be mentioned that it is also exposed to a back-of-the-harbour wind; westerly gales find their way from Peel along the valleys and fall on the harbour quite sharply. A temporary berth can be found on the Battery Pier with the trawlers, but it is rather a rough place.

I always chose the third possibility, that of going into the inner harbour which is tidal, even if it means waiting for water; the Harbour Master will swing the new footbridge when requested. Here the initial berths to starboard are commercial, but beyond them yachts moor in tiers or to an inactive trawler. There may also be a berth in the Tongue, used mainly by local boats; here one dries out to level sand, being usually undisturbed in the centre of the town. The town itself, while often crowded, has full supplies; there is plenty to do and see including the TT races, steam trains, and an electric tramway along the coast to Ramsey and up to Snaefell.

### The Langness Complex

See Chart No 2094 and the plan in Chart No 2696. After having exhausted the attractions of the capital city, it is proposed to circumnavigate the island clockwise. Leaving Douglas then around HW, the stream should serve to carry the boat round the Calf and reach Peel. It is however more interesting if calls are made at intermediate places. On the coastwise passage to Langness three little ports – Soderick, Grenaugh and Solderick – can be identified from the chart. These are three Viking named, open landing places, said to have been used for smuggling but there is little of interest ashore. After rounding Santon Head (with Baltic Rock off-lying), Derby Haven is marked by St Michael's Island to seaward and King William's College and Ronaldsway Airport ashore.

### Derby Haven

See Chart No 2696 for plan. The harbour is said to have been named and used by the Stanley family when they were Lords of Man, and the original Derby horserace was run on a course on Langness before being taken to Epsom. There are no hazards in the approach to the outer harbour and plenty of room for anchorage. Under St Michael's Island the Harbour Board have laid moorings which are leased to private owners and rather jealously guarded; nonetheless it is usually possible to find vacancies for an overnight stay. Though there is shelter from most quarters, a NE gale will sweep straight in. There is a stone slip and a good hotel ashore, otherwise the place is rather isolated with the nearest supplies at Castletown two miles away.

Though there are a number of light shallow draught moorings in the inner harbour, they are not advisable for cruising boats. There is a clear entry between the perch and the end of the breakwater, but the latter is not a quay wall against which boats can tie up; the sandy foreshore is littered with unexpected rocks and, if bad weather came in, the boat would pound. Beyond a small boatyard and chandlery there are no facilities in the village apart from a post box and a bus service.

*Langness*

Moving along the hammerhead of Langness towards the lighthouse is straightforward. At the southern tip however the stream arrows in Chart No 2094 show spring rates of five knots and though no race is charted, in fact the Langness race can be very nasty when, for instance, there is a strong south-westerly over the tide. In the daytime this can be avoided by standing out and round, but at night it is only sensible to keep well out and not alter until the Calf light shows – see Chart No 2094. Once round Langness Point proper, the mid-bay buoy (lit), and the lit entry to Castletown show.

*Castletown*

The passage across Castletown Bay is notorious for badly marked lobster pots, and the place seems littered with rocks, but keeping close to the red can buoy is the answer. The charted anchorage is for ships, yachts can move further in to wait for water where, though the bay is fully open to the south, it is sheltered from most other quarters. There is yacht anchorage off the entry in fair shelter (kelp) though wind can come across the neck of the isthmus. Incidentally the name of Ronaldsway is said to have come from one Ronald who portaged his Viking ship across the neck

Fig. 9 Langness.

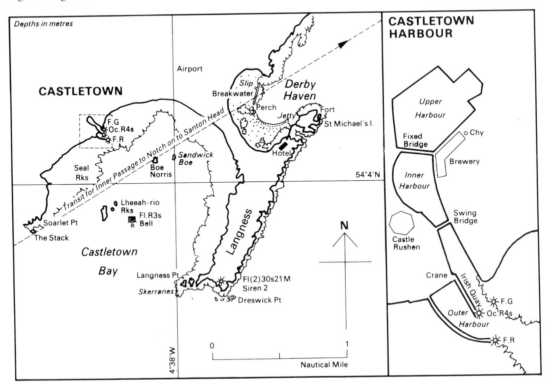

after being annoyed by the Langness race. At the moment there is little or no commercial or trawler traffic using the harbour, and the previous container crane has now been struck down. Enter at half flood and exit before half ebb.

There are at Castletown four harbours in series, that can best be seen in the aerial photograph taken on the run-in to the airport. The breakwater encircles the outer harbour which looks inviting at HW, being quayed round with a slip; it is usually empty and unused because it accepts swell and, like the whole system, dries. Pass this by and entering between the lit port and starboard perches, the Irish Quay presents, running to the swing footbridge. This is the commercial berth and used to have container traffic with Glasson Dock and Preston, but this has been given up. It is best to tie up initially here and consult the Harbour Master whose office is on the quay above. Administration is from Port St Mary but the deputy, who controls both Castletown and Derby Haven, is very helpful. At neaps it is possible to lie afloat at the steps just before the swing footbridge, thus avoiding the need to rouse out the key man to open this.

When the inner harbour is full, it must be admitted that it looks like a well contrived setting for a water pageant. When ebbed it dries to a clean sandy bottom as do most of the island's inner harbours. In the sunlight the swans swim with great

*Castletown*. The four harbours are shown together with the swing footbridge and the fixed road bridge. *Author*

*Chicken Rock*. This lighthouse and its attendant dangers need to be given a good berth. *Author*

dignity. The left hand quay is dominated by the brooding Rushen Castle – the seat of the Manx government until 1874. The right is taken up by the harmonising Castletown brewery, with the Glue Pot pub in one corner. Berthing is to either quay though ladders are scanty and it may be necessary to tie up outside a local boat. There is complete shelter and peaceful sanctuary apart from some take-off noise from the airport. The great drawback to the harbour is that it gives rise to much reluctance to go back to sea. The upper harbour is closed off, except for mastless craft, by a fixed road bridge.

The small town offers full supplies and some marine services. There is a steam railway line running to Port Erin and to Douglas, and the airport is on the doorstep; both Castle Rushen and the maritime museum call for visits. By taking to the dinghy there is excellent sea fishing in Castletown Bay. It is surprising to me that so few cruising boats come into the harbour and that there is little yachting activity and no sailing club – perhaps due to competition from Port St Mary.

70

**The Calf Complex**

The south-west tip of the Isle of Man is marked by a group of small islands, the chief of which are the Calf and Chicken Rock, the former with a powerful lighthouse and the latter with a weaker one on a tall tower (which makes a good daymark).

*Port St Mary*

See Chart No 2094 and plan in Chart No 2696. This harbour has long been the favourite port of entry for yachts, largely due to the activity and hospitality of the Isle of Man SC. In daylight the approach is open, but coming from the south one is apt to be misled and head for the more obvious Castletown as Port St Mary is rather tucked away round Kallow Point. The only hazard is the Carrick Rock, a lit beacon difficult to pick up against the shore; moreover, the light being difficult to maintain, may not be working. Apart from the pier head lights, there is behind the harbour a red lit four hundred feet high radio mast which may be visible above low mist. Cregneish RDF beacon is on high ground overlooking the harbour. There is an outer and inner harbour with moorings and anchorage off.

With winds round north and south the shelter is good. Winds from east and north east come straight in and circle, making both outer moorings and anchorage uncomfortable or impossible. But more frequent and more troublesome is the back-of-the-harbour wind, which in my experience can make HW at the outer wall very trying. North-westerly gales funnel from Fleshwick Bay, cross the col, and drop

*Port St Mary*. There is water to the base of the outer harbour wall, where there is a lifeboat slip. The inner harbour dries to the tip of the wall at springs. *Author*

down hard on the harbour; similarly south-westerlies cross from Port Erin. Their effect in the inner harbour is less.

In the near approach note that the beacon on Carthure Rocks may have been flattened by the last easterly gale. It is best to give the outer pier-head a good berth, then come in slowly and make fast initially to one of the trawlers. This is an active fishing port with the home boats going out after the morning forecast and returning in the evening, so that an overnight berth here is emphatically to be avoided. There is water at all times along the outer wall, but at this stage it is best to look round and talk to the Harbour Master about a choice of berth. Recently the water alongside the top of the wall has been deepened to 2.5m (8 ft) at LWS but, after the iron beacon on the spoil bank, the passage is only 100 ft wide up to the last set of steps. This is a favoured and sheltered berth for yachts to lie afloat (the trawlers not intruding) but space may be tight. There is a drop of twenty plus feet (6m) at low water, calling for long lines and a watchful eye on the boat.

Drying out in the inner harbour is satisfactory, but one will not float till half flood. Either anchor in the middle on clean firm sand or tie up outside an inactive boat at the wall – check the draught and overhangs of the inside boat, and put out own warps ashore. In the aerial photograph can be seen the visitor's moorings and anchorage area; there can be difficulty for boats here in strong weather. Donald the dolphin used to add to the problems of dinghy work here, but he has now finally left Port St Mary and is popular in Falmouth.

Like most little places in the Island there is a nostalgic air of Victorian times about this harbour and its surroundings; one can even catch the reek of peat smoke. There are still the same simple amusements such as walking, fishing in the bay and golf.

## Calf Sound

See Plan on Chart No 2696. The temptation to use the Sound is that it saves six miles in contrast to going round by Chicken Rock, and even longer if a wide sweep has to be made. It has however a deservedly bad reputation with local people who are reluctant to give visitors advice on it. At the right time and under the right conditions it is placid and easy. If committed to the passage in the wrong conditions, the only consolation is that boats are usually spewed out unhurt.

*Navigation*   The actual sound is narrow (about 750 ft), short (about 1,200 ft), and deep (about 80 ft at HWS) which gives a large volume of passing water. The stream in fact is charted as 3.5 knts maximum but could easily reach 5 knts. Stream reversal is out of step with high and low water round the IOM: that to the south runs from two hours before LW to one and half hours before HW; it then reverses to north-going, with probably little or no slack water period. Wind strength and direction are critical factors since, with this stream rate, rough water is to be expected. Wind with tide will give hollow curling waves, while wind over tide will give irregular standing waves. When coming from the east, it is possible to look into the Sound and then turn away, but this may not be possible when romping in from

72

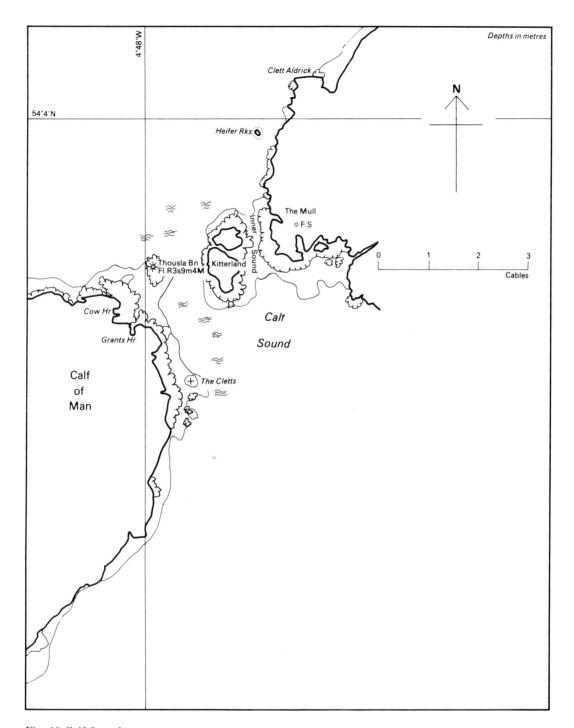

**N**

4°48'W

54°4'N

Clett Aldrick

Heifer Rks

The Mull
○ F.S

Inner Sound

Thousla Bn
Fl.R3s9m4M

Kitterland

Calf
Sound

Cow Hr

Grants Hr

Calf
of
Man

⊕ The Cletts

0    1    2    3

Cables

Fig. 10 Calf Sound.

*Calf Sound.* From the north west. To starboard Thoulsa Island with beacon. *Author*

the west side with a strong following wind. Yachts and trawlers coming through with the tide under them sheer about and are not under good control. It is best to hang back until the pass is clear. Clearly no attempt should be made to use the Sound in fog.

The leading mark is that old favourite Thousla beacon, conspic, and painted in fading red. 'Thousla is mothered by the Calf, do not come between mother and daughter.' In other words, leave the beacon close to port. There is recent notification that the beacon has been given a flashing red light and, though this would not tempt me to run the Sound at night, trawlers would do this. The resident cormorant is often to be seen drying its wings on the beacon giving a spreadeagle top mark.

In nipping round to the other side of the Island I have never found any trouble in Calf sound, because it has always been possible to choose the right conditions and

74

the right timing. From the inner harbour at Peel, with the need to wait for water to start, the timing will be late. In the long distance approach from Ireland, Holyhead and so on, the ETA cannot be guaranteed, and in such cases the course should be laid to pass outside the Chicken Rock. As with the other strong sounds in the Irish Sea, they can all be passed in safety at the right time.

## Chicken Rock

Use Chart No 2094. Like the Point of Ayre there is no plan, but a sketch map has been provided here. It is a pinnacle rock which was a great scourge to the old sailing ships because it was almost impossible to light it. Initially Stevenson overcame this by putting two lighthouses on the Calf, transitting the Rock's position; later he managed to build a tall lighthouse tower which is a magnificent daymark. This is

Fig. 11 Chicken Rock.

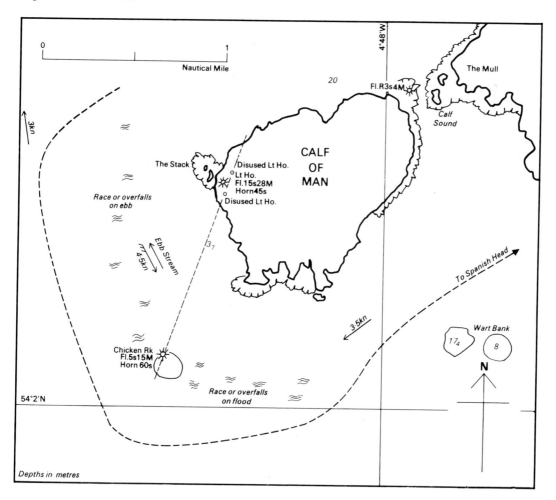

now unmanned and it should be carefully noted that its intensity is little more than that of a buoy. Coming from the west at night it would be a serious mistake to read the grand new Calf light as that of Chicken Rock. The majority of the north-going spring flood stream, which reaches at least five knots, is diverted to the east coast of the main Island, giving races round the Rock. The equally strong ebb stream which is so often running against the prevalent south-westerlies, gives rough water and calls for a wide berth. The cognoscenti speak of 'The Chickens', suggesting that it is a haunt of Mother Carey's brood.

On the Calf, the towers of Stevenson's two original (now disused) lighthouses lie one each side of the new lighthouse; this, being faced with natural stone, is less easily picked up from seaward. The obscured sectors of the Calf light should be carefully studied on the chart; it will be seen that the light is invisible along the whole of the west coast and to a large extent to the east. What is needed by the yachtsman is a light on Contrary Head, but there is too little commercial traffic to warrant this.

Having rounded Chicken Rock and the Calf from the east, it is important to lay a course on Bradda Head and not cut straight into Port Erin, as this would cross the sunken breakwater in the approach. Formerly the Calf supported a small population but it is now a bird sanctuary with the only residents a warden and the lighthouse keepers; there are only boat landings and no anchorage. Those who wish to visit can best do this by using the daily trips from the Raglan Pier at Port Erin. Coming now on to the west coast, it is easy to see why yachts do not explore it. It is mostly lined by iron-bound cliffs carrying memories of fierce blows from south west to north. It is sparsely populated with the only harbour at Peel. The ferry from Liverpool occasionally goes round to Peel when strong easterly weather shuts Douglas, and the rare trawler is to be seen. There are no lights, though the Niarbyl is the only inshore hazard.


*Port Erin*
See Chart No 2094 and plan in Chart No 2696. This is a delightful seaside resort, and the gently curving bay sheltering under Bradda Head should attract yachtsmen. This it notably fails to do and the empty bay is devoid of yacht moorings. There are two heavy visitor's moorings but these too are rarely in use, though in settled weather one can spend a quiet night there. It is fatally open from round SW to beyond NW, whence comes all the heavy weather. Leading lights and marks on shore show the safe way in, and the charted line of the under-water cable warns against anchoring in its vicinity. Raglan Pier dries, but offers some fair shelter outside or inside the local fishing boats if a berth can be negotiated. The sunken breakwater offers a stern lesson on the frailty of man's puny efforts and the small unlit black conical buoy must never be passed except on the outside. This full-size pier was built in 1864 but was overwhelmed by a gale before it was even opened officially by Queen Victoria. It is of course charted and revealed by my aerial

*Port Erin*. Note the ruined breakwater which lies across a direct approach from the south. *Author*

photograph taken at low water, but at night it is all too easy for a boat to head straight into the bay; one must hold on until the leading lights are in line.

In settled easterly weather and sunshine Port Erin is a grand place provided the forecasts are watched. There is bathing, fishing, golf, and the Marine Biological Station, while Port St Mary is two miles away, and Douglas accessible by the railway.

### The West Coast of the Isle of Man

See Chart No 2094. Apart from Peel, there is no shelter between Port St Mary and Ramsey on this trip, so the forecasts should be watched carefully, as the overall distance is thirty-five to forty miles. The tidesmeet is at Contrary Head and the stream is slack in both directions from here. Bradda Head has a good daymark in Milner's Tower with the outline shape of a safe key. Beyond is Bradda Hill (which often makes a cloud plume to fall on Port St Mary), with below it Fleshwick Bay,

77

which is a gloomy solitary place open to the north, really only a boat landing and there is nothing ashore. Port Erin offers similar but much better accommodation. Further along the forbidding cliffs there is the unpublicised Niarbyl reef. This projects about a third to half a mile, coming as a surprise packet since it has no beacon. In the small rocky bay to its south there is boat landing. By now Contrary Head is visible and identified by the well named pimple of Corrin's Folly. Peel is hidden by Contrary Hill but at last opens clear to the castle. The history of Mr Corrin's tower is an involved story of 19th century sectarianism.

*Peel*

Chart No 2904 and Plan in No 2696. The overall picture is well shown by my aerial photograph. The entry is quite open but so is the exposure from round north so that, despite the secondary breakwater, the inner side of the outer breakwater can be very uncomfortable. Approaching from the NW, Peel is not easy to pick up as mist collects in its valley. The whole of the west elevation of the island is clear, as is the low lying northern plain but there is no radiobeacon except over the hills at Douglas.

Though exposed from a rather too wide arc, there is water at the outer breakwater at all states. It is however busy with trawlers, particularly in the herring

*Peel.* Corrins Folly sits atop Contrary Head. The outer wall of the harbour is based on St Patrick's Isle, with its ruined castle. The tidal harbour is quayed round. *Author*

season when boats also come into the inner harbour to barrel their catch (ungutted) in brine. It is good for an overnight stay and perhaps in westerly weather for longer. It is best to come as far up to the inshore end as possible and tie outside an inactive trawler – the skippers will advise. Anchorage is also possible by the inner breakwater beacon, but with a change in the wind to NW, the berth can become very exposed. The comfort and complete shelter of the inner harbour is to be preferred every time.

The inner harbour has water to enter three hours each side of HW, and dries to clean level sand, through which the stream of the Neb trickles. There is a large sheet of water nearly half a mile in length which is quayed all round, the Town Quay to port being the most convenient and sunnier side. Beyond the Harbour Master's office, a notice reserves the first part of the quay for trawlers. Further on one can tie up outside a heavier boat and watch how one's own dries down. Keel boats will find more clear wall space on the opposite side of the harbour. It is unusual for the inner harbour to accept any significant swell.

There is plenty to do and see in and around the town, even though in the busy season the draught beer can be variable in quality. Supplies and services are good. There is riding, seafishing, golf and swimming, as well as a climb to Corrin's Folly and exploration of St Patrick's Isle.

## The Point of Ayre

See Chart No 2094 and Sketch Map. Note that the Point of Air is in Wales at the mouth of the River Dee. Northwards from Peel it is a matter of eighteen miles to the Point and another six to Ramsey without any shelter. A lee shore without any refuge, so that it might be worth getting a local forecast from the Ronaldsway Met Office before setting out. The tidal stream is easy until reaching the Point. After leaving Peel, the cliffs gradually fade to that most remarkable island feature – the northern plain – in marked contrast to the mountains of most of the island. This is thought to result from the remains of an Ice Age glacier, hence its composition of boulder clay and gravel. The Norse name for gravel is Ayres and the gravel elevators at the Point are even more conspic than the lighthouse. The coastline on this leg is featureless with only low clay cliffs. Jurby airfield is now closed, but a Nato bombing range is operational at times, though the main target buoys lie three miles out to sea, enabling one to pass inshore. Should there be any activity, there will be a guard boat on duty. Jurby Head, Blue Point and Rue Point do not stand out and are difficult to identify.

Though in settled weather the Point of Ayre can be rounded easily given the right timing, the yachtsman can on occasions find it an unpleasant place. Mainly because he is strictly confined to a close inshore course by the Strunakill Bank (The Strews) to the west and the Whitestone Bank on the east side. Slipping along by the gravel foreshore the need for the Low Light is clear, though coming round at night is inadvisable, as one cannot see where the rough water lies. The south-going flood stream divides here, the eastern element being the stronger, and it is best to come

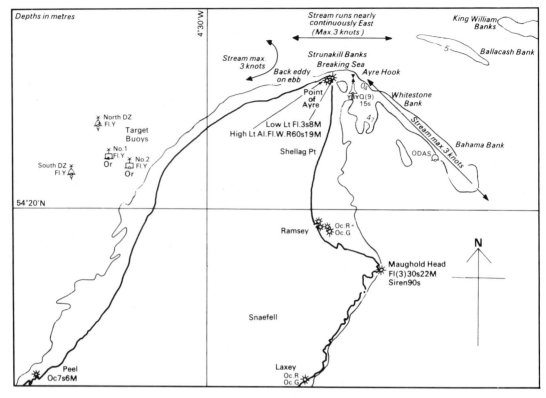

Depths in metres

4°30'W

Stream runs nearly
continuously East
(Max.3 knots)

King William
Banks

Ballacash Bank

5

Stream max.
3 knots

Strunakill Banks
Breaking Sea

Back eddy
on ebb

Ayre Hook

Point
of
Ayre

Whitestone
Bank

Q(9)
15s

North DZ
Fl.Y

Target
Buoys

Low Lt Fl.3s8M
High Lt Al.Fl.W.R60s19M

Bahama Bank

ODAS

Shellag Pt

No.1
Fl.Y

No.2
Fl.Y

South DZ
Fl.Y

Or

Or

54°20'N

Stream max. 3 knots

Ramsey

Oc.R +
Oc.G

N

Maughold Head
Fl(3)30s22M
Siren90s

Snaefell

Peel
Oc7s6M

Laxey
Oc.R
Oc.G

Fig. 12 Point of Ayre.

round at slack water. Strong wind from any quarter puts a gloss on the unpleasantness, while the chief trouble spot is the passage inshore of the Whitestone Bank buoy. Not many yachtsmen actually round the point, but many pass going to or coming from, the Mull of Galloway (there is an RDF station at the lighthouse). Coming from Ramsey it is easy enough to reach the Point at HW slack, but on a longer approach the ETA cannot be so well timed. In which case in heavy weather it is best to divert to Peel rather than consider the longer course outside the Bahama Bank. In emphasing the hazards of the Point of Ayre it should be said that I have personally had no problems there, but have been guided by the harrowing stories of my friends who have hit it at the wrong time in poor weather.

**Ramsey**
See Chart No 2094 and Plan in Chart No 2696. Once past the Point of Ayre, passage across Ramsey Bay excites no comment. Its presence is heralded by hotels and boarding houses, and now by a high rise block of flats. If it is proposed to anchor off, it is best to do this north of the harbour entry and as close into the beach as possible. Anything south of this may be in the trawler fairway and a riding light is

80

*Ramsey*. At the bottom of the picture is the condemned steamer pier. The entry channel, inner harbour and swing bridge can all be seen at the top; the harbour entrance is dry at low water. *Author*

necessary (though not always full protection). Because the harbour is tidal, there is no home trawler fleet but in the herring season the catch is brought in for barrelling. In practice, anchoring off is a fair guarantee for a rolling berth, as the bay is wide open to the NE sector – it may suffice for a night stop-over and allow one to get away at any state.

The Queen's Pier was built for excursion steamers but is now condemned and has been out of use for years; yachtsmen should avoid making any use of it and it offers no shelter. The previously charted yacht moorings have been removed and the pier structure is so decrepid as to be dangerous to use even for landing. It is still lit and provides good rod fishing, but only expense prevents its necessary removal.

It can be seen from the aerial photograph that the two entry piers ensure a completely protected harbour but dry out to the tips; there is water to enter after half flood. At the top of the entry channel there is a beach for multihulls to dry out inside the starboard hand lit beacon – see photograph. This also shows the yacht berths (Nos 4 and 5 on chart) against the Town Quay. It is very pleasant indeed to

81

*Ramsey*. Berthing to the quay. The swing bridge can just be made out to the right of the picture. *Author*

come in at HW and step right onto the quay, and be welcomed by six pubs as well as being right in the centre of the town. Boats lie in trots outside each other and it is essential to add one's own warps to the cat's cradle already there. From half ebb onwards there is quite a different picture. There is a firm level sandy bottom ideal for a scrub down, but keel boats are notorious for falling over and out, usually in the night; they can also fall in if not settled down right. Local boats go under or through the swing bridge where there is a boat yard.

Ramsey provides all facilities and supplies and the Manx C and SC is close at hand. The Ramsey Coastguard is the chief station on the island being continuously manned and having a far reaching aerial on Snaefell. This peak can be reached by the electric railway (change at Laxey Junction), but there is no point in the exercise if it can be seen that Manaman's Mantle is sitting on the top.

*Laxey*. The sheltered entry under Laxey Head. There is a long run in behind the wall, and the inner harbour is half hidden behind the old warehouse. *Author*

## Laxey

See Chart No 2904; there is no plan. Sheltering under Laxey Head, this harbour is quite the prettiest in the island and is well sheltered. It is however so small and crowded that a visitor would not be able to raise a berth, and must content himself with looking in and tying along the port hand entry wall for a few hours at the top end of the tide (the whole harbour dries); it is well worth doing this. In the approach from Maughold (pronounced Maccull) Head, Laxey remains hidden until one is abeam and there are many lobster pots to contend with. Inside the starboard hand wall there are possible berths; however, not only is this exposed but the bottom is rocky and irregular. On the starboard hand of the inside approach there are puzzling beacons; these mark a training wall which diverts the river out of the harbour to diminish silting. At the head of the port hand wall there are steps and temporary

83

*Laxey*. The approach channel showing the covering training wall marked by beacons. *Author*

berthing. Beyond this the crowded inner harbour opens. There is no trawler or coaster traffic here and even the monthly visit of the grain boat has now been discontinued (the grain now comes to the mill by road).

Originally Laxey exported the silver, lead and copper from the mines in the hills with storage in the big warehouse on the quay. Meerschaum pipes are now made there, with sale of the seconds or rejects during the summer. The river was used for water power and weaving. The road can be climbed to the electric railway station, while a further walk will take one to the Laxey Wheel used for pumping the mines. This has now been restored to working order.

Between Laxey and Douglas there are no further harbours, and the coastline shows no significant cruising features in the completion of the circumnavigation.

## IX    Morecambe — Conway

**Charts**

| No | Title | Scale 1: |
|----|-------|----------|
| 1121 | Irish Sea with St George's Channel and North Channel. | 500,000 |
| 1951 | Approaches to Liverpool. | 25,000 |
| 1978 | Great Ormes Head to Liverpool. | 75,000 |
| 1981 | Approaches to Preston. | 75,000 |
| | Preston docks. | 10,000 |
| 3477 | Port of Liverpool – southern part. | 12,500 |
| 3478 | Manchester Ship Canal and upper Mersey. | 25,000 |
| | Manchester docks; Runcorn and Weston docks. | 10,000 |
| | Ellesmere Port and Stanlow oil docks. | 10,000 |
| 3490 | Port of Liverpool – northern part. | 12,500 |

**Morecambe Bay to the Mersey**

See overall Chart No 1121. In returning from the trip to the Isle of Man, boats from the Morecambe Bay clubs usually take a course from Ramsey to the Lune Deep buoy while the Mersey fleet sail from Port St Mary to the Bar. The winds for the return are usually favourable from the NW while the streams are not strong, as they set into Liverpool and Morecambe Bays. The depth contours lend some support to the idea that the Isle of Man was at one time attached to the Lancashire coast. Luckily the courses do not call for crossing Bahama, Ballacash or King William Banks, for strong winds throw up rough water here. Between Walney Island and the Skerries on Anglesey there are no marine radiobeacons, but Blackpool (BPL) and Wallasey (WAL) come in clearly as guides.

*Blackpool*

Use Chart No 1981. Resuming the journey to the south and coming out of Morecambe Bay, the chart will suggest the need to avoid Rossall Patches. This rocky bastion to the south of the bay is a rough unfriendly place, as is the whole Blackpool shore. My policy is to make out to the Shell Wharf buoy before turning to the south. There is of course no suspicion of a harbour at Blackpool, though in fair weather one can anchor off the shore and row in to the famous sands or land at one of the piers; with an offshore wind the smell of hot dogs is pervasive miles out to sea. In low mist or fog it is possible to see the top of Blackpool Tower (180m or 600 feet) showing through above.

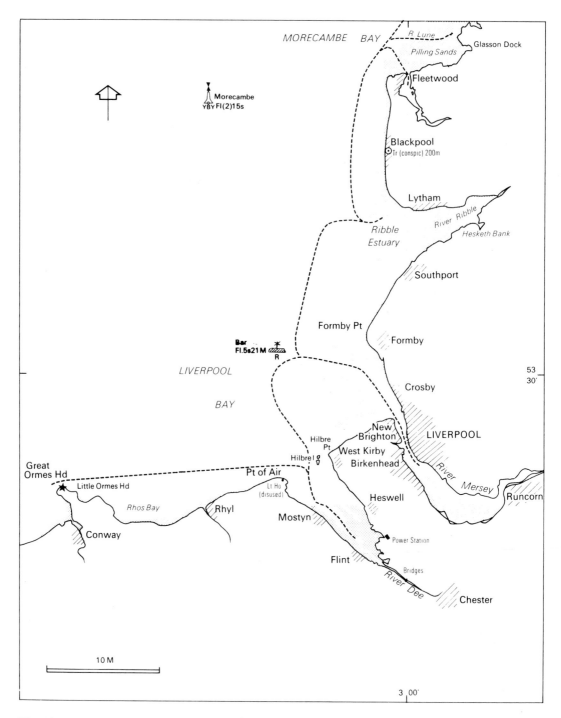

Fig. 13 Morecambe Bay to Conway.

86

Bog Hole

*Southport.* Drying moorings in the Bog Hole. *Author*

## Southport

In Chart No 1981 this resort lies on the south bank of the Ribble estuary. It could hardly ever have been a port, but fishing boats lay to heavy trots along the pleasure pier to which steamers once came. The half tide entry across the banks is perched by the West Lancs SC, who have a clubhouse on the Marine Lake. There are a handful of drying moorings in the Bog Hole (see aerial photograph); they are very exposed from the NW. Landing can be made at the Pierhead and a train can be taken to the mainland.

## The River Ribble

This is fully laid out in Chart No 1981. There must be some fatal significance in the chart number, since the year 1981 saw the death of Preston as a port. After centuries of trading, and just as the Morecambe gas field might have prolonged its life, the navigation has been closed as quite uneconomic. Preston lies fourteen miles from the Gut fairway buoy due to a large delta. The distant fairway buoy of Nelson is an important mark which is still in operation, though some change in position or form is forecast. Going north on a clear night, one can carry its pinprick until the light of the Lune Deep buoy is picked up.

The original channel needed constant dredging, repairing of walls and many lit buoys and beacons, which have now been abandoned or withdrawn, though at the time of writing they are still featured on the chart dated 1979 and a new edition is awaited. So that now the Preston Dock, two thousand feet in length and with an intact lock, is empty but for the pilot boat and dredger and the large dock estate is vacant. Again it is a natural for a yacht marina provided that the channel is marked. Preston is trying to attract a developer and the issue is in the balance, but at the moment the river is not suitable for visitors.

Six miles up river from the Gut buoy and just short of the restored windmill, is the prominent clubhouse of the Ribble Cruising Club. There is a good slip here and visiting yachtsmen are welcome; however the moorings not only dry to mud but are widely exposed from south to NW. The club berths are well sheltered in the creek of Lytham Port a little higher up, where the boats dry to floating stages. The entry is well posted and there are services and supplies nearby.

Higher up again on the north side there is a boatyard in the creek at Freckleton. At the same level but on the opposite shore there is perched entry to the River Douglas which, after a twisty three or four miles, arrives at Hesketh Bank or Tarleton. The passage needs careful timing as for much of the tide the river is a deep sided muddy ditch; there is entry and a lock to the much weeded canal here. At the Hesketh Bank boatyard yachts moor to stagings or lay up out of the water for winter.

### The River Mersey

See Chart No 1951, for approaches and Queen's and Crosby channels. Charts Nos 3477 and 3490 cover the actual port. It might be supposed that this big river and erstwhile great port of Liverpool would be a yachtsman's Mecca, but this is far from the case; it is simply a port for big ships, while yacht clubs are centres of enthusiasm surviving despite very poor conditions. Coming into the river on a spring flood backed by a strong north-westerly is to see these to the full. There were originally three entrances through the delta: the Formby channel from the north – this is now sanded up; The Rock channel from the SW – this is still viable round the top of the tide and perched by local clubs, but not advisable for visitors; the main channel (Queen's and Crosby) is deep, well lit and controlled by the Port Radar station at Seaforth. There is a high rise and strong stream notably at the Liverpool Pierhead – thirty plus fee (9m) with storm surges and five to six knots of rate at springs.

The outer mark is the Bar buoy, with a high focal plane light of such intensity that it is not only blinding by night, but is also visible for about ten miles in daylight! The bar is a rough place, the haunt of anchored ships awaiting entry. The named Fairway buoy lies further in, but is still a distance of ten miles from the first docks.

When commercial traffic is moving in the channel yachts must keep out of the way – with the tide astern and only half the channel available, a ship cannot effectively slow or alter course. On the other hand there is mostly room for yachts to dodge outside the channel buoys and choose the moment to put in a tack.

The long approach channel becomes rather monotonous as the buoys number off; these may not conform to those shown in an unamended 1976 edition of the chart as some were removed in 1981. The revetment walls can be crossed by a yacht after three or four hours flood. The first moorings on the way in are those of the Blundellsands SC in the River Alt, south of Hightown; the sands can be crossed two hours each side of HW, leaving the channel at C 14 buoy. Visitors who are brave enough to attempt the entry should do so on the flood, aiming for the two basket poles on the marked sewer wall and leaving them to starboard. There are perches, difficult to interpret, but the line of boats in the Alt will now be in view. The moorings dry but there is a slip and clubhouse, with a laying-up yard at Hightown. Except on a high spring tide and an onshore wind there is shelter behind the banks. In practice, however, unless one can make contact with a BSC boat cruising off to show the way in, the entry is rather too shifting for the casual visitor. Beyond the Blundellsands SC it should be noted that the labelled marina at Crosby is simply a dinghy sailing lake with no access from the sea.

Having passed the disused Rock lighthouse at New Brighton, the river proper has been entered and Chart No 3490 needs careful study in search of a berth. Beyond the truncated New Brighton pier the yacht moorings of the New Brighton SC are charted and further on those of the Wallasey SC; these are now few in number and a sluicing stream runs through them, wearing the ground tackle quickly. There is deep water anchorage here sheltered from the west, but it is necessary to come as close as possible and show an anchor light. The other charted yacht moorings are beyond the Tranmere oil terminal and jointly shared by the Royal Mersey YC and the Tranmere SC. Again the stream runs fast here, with wash from passing ships not to mention oil smells and spills. So that apart from casual anchoring the river itself can offer little comfort to the incoming yacht.

There are miles of docks on the Liverpool side some of which are being abandoned and filled in. A yacht will always be accepted with other in-going traffic, and easily tucked away in some corner; few present themselves and the security is poor. Three dock entrances are maintained: Gladstone, Langston, and Waterloo, the latter being the most suitable. All the South Liverpool docks are now disused but the Brunswick dock entrance has been left permanently open; at low water both the Brunswick and the Coburg show mounds of deep grey mud. Yachts and other small boats come in to berth round HW either against the walls or to moorings; to reach the latter when there is no water the natives resort to 'quanting' the dingy like a sledge across the mud. The dock area is decayed and vandalised (Toxteth is close inland). There is of course full shelter, but it is hardly attractive for visitors.

For a stay in the Mersey for more than a day or two, it is best to enter the Wallasey docks by the Alfred Dock entrance. With little commercial traffic, acres of water and miles of quay space, the system acts like a marina and welcomes yachts. It is possible to get in touch with the Dockmaster by radio to advise arrival, but the skipper will have to climb up to the office on the downstream knuckle to sign papers and be allocated a berth. Just at the entrance there is an indent for anchoring out of the fairway. The entry lies between the Wallasey and Birkenhead ferry landing stages; there are twin entry locks via which vessels can enter four hours each side of HW. In the lock there is a large rise and fall with only a single ladder to hold on to and take up warps; yachts usually have to pass when larger traffic is using the lock. It is necessary to wait till a busy road bridge swings before being able to leave the Alfred Dock, and it must be remembered that on exit there may be a stream of up to five knots to deal with – i.e. the engine mustn't fail. The dock area is as usual decayed and insecure country, so that a berth close to the new Police Station at Egerton Dock has advantages. Nearby supplies are poor, but within a few hundred yards the Hamilton Square underground connects with Liverpool.

The upper reaches of the River Mersey are shown in Chart No 3477 and the Manchester Ship Canal in No 3478. The topography is shaped like a large flask of a drying inland lagoon. It is the filling and emptying of this that not only sweeps the channel but sets up the fierce streams which plague the river. On the north bank the Garston Channel is still operational but Garston has nothing to offer the yachtsman. A little further up, the Liverpool SC offers dinghy sailing on the tide, but here the natives roam the beach with guns. The navigation to Runcorn has been withdrawn. On the opposite bank, the Eastham Channel takes ship traffic to the Eastham Locks and the Ship Canal; yachts use this when making for the Weaver and associated inland waters.

### The Dee Estuary

See Chart No 1978, there is no larger scale information. To the east of a line between West Kirby and Mostyn Quay there is no detailed chartwork and only the general outline is shown. Buoyage west of this line is under the accepted aegis of Trinity House but, though the channel east of Mostyn is buoyed, no marks are shown. The whole area is a mass of drying sand but with well marked channels for yachts. Perhaps the most significant feature is that the estuary is guarded to seaward by the Hoyle Banks (East and West) which dry in places to seven metres (23 ft), thus giving shelter through much of the tide cycle. The estuary is therefore not approached direct, but by Hilre Swash from the north and by the Welsh Channel from the south. In any heavy wind the Hoyle Banks cannot be crossed.

Assuming a course from the Mersey, the question is at what point to leave the channel. Local boats will use what remains of the Rock Channel, turning to the west at the Brazil buoy before the revetment wall starts (there are locally sited perches); boats from the Blundellsands Sailing Club wait till four hours flood, when there is water to cross the revetment and the Burbo Bank. The orthodox exit will be to leave the channel after Q9 and head south to pick up HE2 buoy. The Hilbre channel is well marked and lit, with water at all states, being used by small coasters making for Mostyn. This is followed to the Welshman buoy past Hibre Island and the seal colony on the W Hoyle Bank opposite. At this point there is a sand harbour with good shelter until the banks uncover. Welshman's Gut leads to the west, but the main channel continues past Seldom Seen buoy which is marked, and the East Bar and Caldy buoys which are not charted; this leads to Dawpool with Sally's Cottage on the shore. Here there are moorings and often enough water for a boat to remain afloat with fair shelter under the banks. A strong slip has been built across the shore, and the Heswal SC is proposing to build a clubhouse here. Higher up and needing a spring tide, is a small boat-yard where boats may be laid up. Beyond Heswall the old main channel to Parkgate has filled up and any channel to the opposite bank has vanished.

## Hoylake

Chart No 1978. This very old harbour has now completely lost the original Hoyle Lake which provided shelter, but it is accessible at HW from the Hilbre channel, the E Hoyle Bank drying to eight metres (26 ft). The Hoylake SC have their clubhouse on the promenade, and there are many moorings for yachts and other boats which dry out to mud or sand on the foreshore; when the banks uncover the north-westerly aspect ensures that gales come straight in and boats frequently break adrift. While it is true that boats are safe from the elements by being dried out for long periods, this in its turn exposes them to vandalism. Even in bilge keels boats it seems doubtful that visitors would be happy here except in settled off shore weather.

## West Kirby

This companion club to Hoylake is further to the south round Hilbre Point, with the clubhouse at the SE end of the Marine Lake; the lake is used for dinghy sailing and it is proposed to extend it. The moorings are much the same as at Hoylake, i.e. drying to mud with marked exposure when the West Hoyle Bank covers. There is however water to anchor in the channel near Seldom Seen buoy, in reasonable comfort for much of the tide, but there is a broad muddy foreshore to negotiate. Crews of the moored boats are put on board by tractor before they float, it is then essential to pick up the moorings again before they dry, and wait until the tractor can come again. There is a good deal of racing activity, but on the whole the cruising boats tend to go elsewhere for the season, and for the same reason visitors will not find it an attractive place to call. Harry Jones, the WKSC boatman, magnificently saved *Sarahay* last season when she was sinking, after being holed as a result of sitting on a mooring anchor.

## Mostyn Harbour

Chart No 1978. Despite its obvious shortcomings, Mostyn has the importance of offering the only real security from heavy westerly weather in the estuary; it is open from the east (when there will be shelter on the opposite shore). Round HW it is possible to sail direct across the banks by accepting some disturbed water, but the more usual approach is via Welshman's Gut, the Dee Buoy and Mostyn Deep. Half flood is needed, since the water is far from deep and the buoys may be out of position. Wild Road is well named.

Originally the site of the Mostyn ironworks, the strong feature is a rough jetty made of molten slag. The harbour is approached on the seaward side of this, the channel being perched and drying, and the jetty carrying a fixed red light. The harbour is privately owned and operated, and yachts are not particularly welcome except in threatening weather. There are pilots and a Harbour Master, while inshore there is the Mostyn Arms. Supplies are remote, but the harbour has been re-furbished, being used by coasters and the occasional trawler. On the ebb a sudden scouring flush from a hidden reservoir may take one by surprise.

Yachts more usually anchor in the bight upstream of the jetty, where there is a constant eddy, but good shelter round to the NE. Having ridden out a Force 8–9 from the NW one night, I can vouch for the fact that the deep mud would seem to have good holding properties. Except at HW when there is a beach, it is rough work scrambling onto the jetty. It is important to move out while the tide is still making in case of running aground, as the buoys are not always a good guide to the channel.

Exploration further up the river is hampered by lack of charting, and it seems that the only source of information is the Harbour Master or Pilot at Mostyn, the buoys being laid and tended from a sub-depot in the harbour. The channel is used by small ships trading out of Shotton beginning at the S Salisbury buoy. Llannerche-y-mor is the first little inlet with anchorage off in deep water; most of the berthing space has now been taken by a beached ferry boat but there is room for a yacht or two. The channel moves out at Greenfield and passes the sanded harbour of Flint. Beyond Flint is the beginning of the straight cut which canalises the Dee to Chester and boasts quite a bore on spring tides. At Connah's Quay the mast must be lowered as there are three fixed bridges ahead. Arrived at Chester there is anchorage off the Roodee race course but little water at LWS. The really adventurous can then scrape under the Old Dee bridge on a HWS and wait for the weir to cover; then, using the salmon leap steps, can take a shallow draught boat into the upper Dee.

Having regained Mostyn Deep it can be seen from the chart that the Welsh Channel is well buoyed and lit leading to the inner Passage. Here one can pass close inshore seeking the entrance to Rhyl harbour.

### Rhyl

Still working on Chart No 1978, there is no larger scale and no harbour plan or indeed an aerial photograph. It is neccssary to take a glass to the chart. It is unfortunate that between the Point of Air (or Ayr) and Great Ormes Head there is no useful refuge and Rhyl will be inaccessible in heavy onshore winds. The local logistic is that in-coming from either the Dee or the Mersey it is necessary to round the Orme before the flood sets in. There is no near fairway buoy to lead into the harbour, merely the green sewer buoy and a curved training wall with beacons;

92

these should be left to port with water across the sands by four hours flood. The harbour in the mouth of the River Clwyd is small and limited by the road bridge, under which a yacht can be swept by a spring flood. Though it is well sheltered it is crammed with small boats on double ended moorings with a sand bank in the middle; luckily the local sailing club is both hospitable and helpful about a mooring. The quay is short and serves a timber yard. Apart from the hot dog miasma, the local mystery is that dinghies tend to cast themselves adrift on the ebb. The harbour dries completely.

On leaving Rhyl the heading is to the west to Little Orme. Colwyn Bay should be ignored as offering no shelter (the two jetties at Llanddulas are for loading stone and the pier at Rhos is foreshortened). Llandudno Bay is entered beyond Little Ormes Head but it is of very slight yachting value, being widely open to the north and west, and the few moorings laid have to be very heavy. At the same time westerly weather comes across the low-lying neck of the peninsula. It is possible to anchor east of the pier and spend a few hours waiting for the tide but, except in very settled weather, it is not a place to pass the night.

*Great Ormes Head.* The lighthouse clinging to the cliff like a nest, 100m (325 ft) up. *Author*

## Great Ormes Head

Chart No 1978. There is deep water close in to the cliffs without any hazards, but the spring stream runs strong, hence the need to arrive before the flood starts. The lighthouse perches three hundred feet up and has an unusual characteristic of Morse B; this dates back many years to the time that it was built by the Mersey Docks and Harbour Company, and on the older charts it was shown merely as four flashes. Arrived at the pitch of the Orme, one is on the threshold of intriguing cruising ground with several possibilities. To the south across Conway Bay lies the mass of Penmaenmawr and the entrance to Conway. Six miles to the west, Puffin Island can be seen with the entrance to the Menai Strait, while to the NW the coast of Anglesey stretches to Point Lynas. In covering these three choices it is proposed to deal with Conway first, then round Anglesey to Caernarvon next, and finally describe the Menai Strait.

# X   Anglesey and the Menai Strait

**Charts**

| No | Title | Scale 1: |
|----|-------|----------|
| 1413 | Approaches to Holyhead. | 25,000 |
| 1464 | Menai Strait. | 25,000 |
| | The Swellies. | 10,000 |
| 1826 | Irish Sea – eastern part. | 200,000 |
| 1970 | Caernarvon Bay. | 75,000 |
| 1977 | Holyhead to Great Ormes Head. | 75,000 |
| 1978 | Great Ormes Head to Liverpool. | 75,000 |
| 2011 | Holyhead Harbour. | 6,250 |
| Book | *Cruising Guide to Anglesey and Conway* (See bibliography) | |

Anglesey and its anchorages are fully covered by my *Cruising Guide to Anglesey and Conway*, which goes into more detail than can be included in the present book; some of the sketch maps are reproduced here.

**Conway**

In Chart No 1978 the scale for the estuary is small and, though the channel is buoyed, only the fairway buoy and the perch are charted. Though this has been my home port for some years, I have resisted the temptation to refer to it as Conwy in the same conservative way that I have never fallen for the short cut of the Inner Passage. This is from the fall of the Orme, across Conway sands to the perch in the channel, and is used by experienced locals, but the possibility of being neaped on falling tides is a great deterrent.

The orthodox entry depends on locating the fairway buoy, which is elusive and unlit, lying three miles SW of the Orme. Coming in from the direction of Puffin Island, the visual course is from the NE tip to the jagged tooth on Penmaen-bach – see photograph. It is possible to enter at any state and anchor between C 5 and C 7 to wait for water. The ebb runs for seven and half hours with a stream of 5 to 6 knots in the narrows at Deganwy. The sole channel light on the perch is not sufficient to allow entry or exit at night. The buoys are singletons and the working policy is to pass them close. The shallowest part is over the mussel bed at the perch, which latter should be left a hundred yards to port when inward bound. The channel is passable three hours each side of HW, and the optimum time to arrive is five hours flood. A line from the perch to the middle of the bridge span will bring one into the harbour proper, with the fairway to the quay between moored boats. At

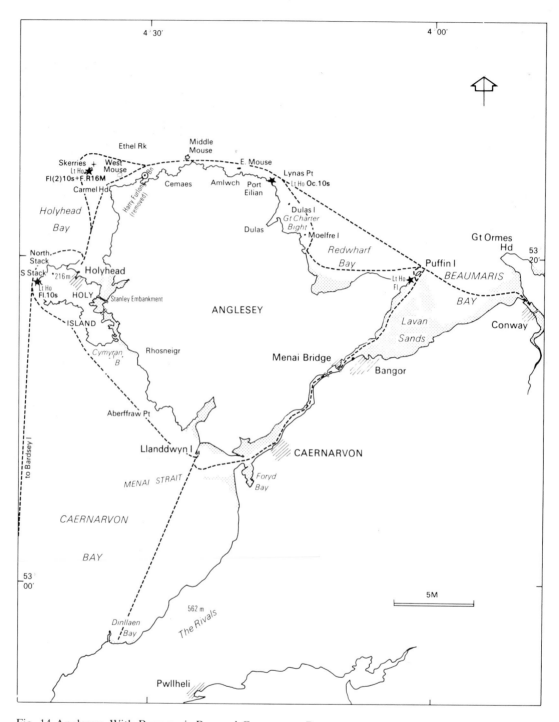

Fig. 14 Anglesey. With Beaumaris Bay and Caernarvon Bay.

*Conway*. The fairway and moorings looking SE, upstream from *Sarahay's* mooring off Bodlondeb Point. *Author*

Fig. 15 Conway.

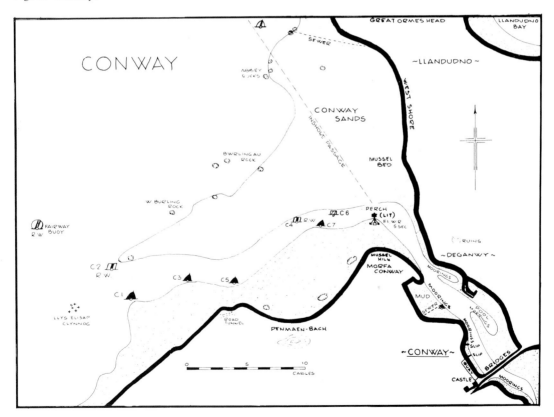

Bodlondeb Point there is a sharp and sudden disconcerting set. Do not attempt to anchor as the bottom is foul with old moorings.

There are four or five hundred moorings in Conway harbour, mostly privately laid and used by boats which are too sensible to leave such a secure base; some dry at half tide. Official trots have been laid in the Pool but these are now not reliable in heavy weather, though one could be picked until enquiries can be made of the boatmen; alternatively a yacht could come up to the quay and enquire of the Harbour Master. There is very good shelter, though NE gales can come in. The fierce stream and the unorganised moorings are the drawbacks from the visitor's point of view.

On the other hand there is no need for me to extol the beauties and attractions of Conway, which have remained largely unchanged since Frank Cowper described them a hundred years ago. Yet over this haven lies a dark impending shadow. An expressway has been deemed necessary from Dublin to Brussels and, while much of the work has been completed, the Conway valley has yet not been crossed. The final plan seems to be to put a trench tunnel across the river from Deganwy to the Morfa. If this open excavation work is carried out, it will mean the complete disruption of

*Conway.* The entry under Penmaen-bach, with the jagged tooth outline on its silhouette, forming a leading mark for the Fairway buoy. *Author*

Jagged tooth

Passing through the channel with fairway buoy 1 M astern

the harbour for several years and most of the present moorings are threatened. As yet no start has been made, but all possible alternatives have been explored and rejected.

## Anglesey

Chart No 1977 covers the whole passage from Conway to Holyhead, a distance of about 35 miles. My usual routine is to cover the whole trip in one tide, but to do this there must be strict attention to the rules. En route, however, there are several small harbours where it is interesting to break the journey; none of these offers complete shelter, while the north coast itself is rock-strewn, poorly lit and quite exposed. But given daylight and good weather, one can make a fast and interesting passage in either direction.

The stream rate is the governing factor. After crossing Holyhead Bay, the flood moves at up to five knots at springs along the coast and into Liverpool Bay. To cover the whole distance within a tide the yacht has to be at either Puffin Island or Carmel Head at slack water – high or low. In addition it is necessary to calculate what the weather will be like along the critical north coast, since a heading wind will make matters unpleasant or impossible. The trip falls into four parts: Conway–Puffin Is, Puffin Is–Point Lynas, Point Lynas–Carmel Head and Carmel Head–Holyhead. To do things neatly it is necessary to keep to schedule at all these points by judicious use of power.

### Conway–Puffin Island

On the first leg, the push comes in getting out of Conway against the flood through the Deganwy narrows, with the spring stream running up to five knots. My boat *Sarahay* has just about a knot in hand under power to do this. Having weathered past the perch, the channel can be a little curtailed at this state of the tide. A course should now be laid on the NE tip of Puffin Island, being careful to avoid being set on to the steep Dutchman's Bank.

*Puffin Island.* Characteristic outline approaching from the west. *Author*

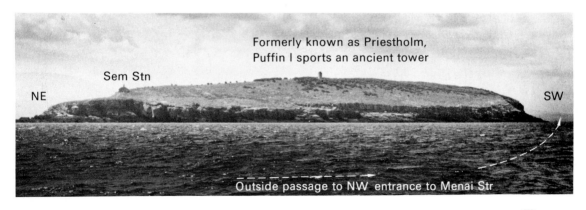

Formerly known as Priestholm,
Puffin I sports an ancient tower

Sem Stn

NE

SW

Outside passage to NW entrance to Menai Str

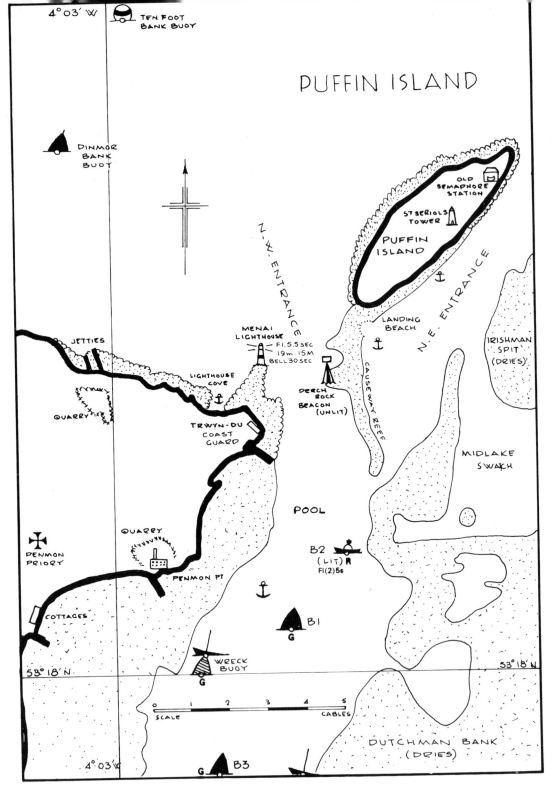

Fig. 16 Puffin Island. With Menai lighthouse.

*Puffin Island*   In side elevation Puffin Island is easily recognised by its two skyline buildings of St Seriol's Tower and the ruined semaphore station at the northern end. Approaching from the direction of Great Ormes head, the end-on view is difficult to pick up, and the lighthouse on Trwyn Du may show first. Vast sandbanks cumber this end of the Straits and none of the swatchways should be used, attention being concentrated on the SW entrance where there is water at all states. The NE entrance is also deep but clearly the long Causeway Reef dries right across its lower end, and once this has been seen at low water, keenness to use the passage dwindles; in any case it is not much longer to use the outside route. There is a rolling uneasy anchorage well under the low cliffs of the SE corner of the island, where a night can be spent in settled weather.

The island itself is a bird sanctuary with no human inhabitants. The birds resent and attack visitors, particularly in the nesting season (and quite right too), while rats have almost wiped out the puffins. There is a landing beach (permission required) at the SW tip on the inshore side. Centuries ago St Seriol built his hermitage here, and this was linked with the still-extant church at Penmon. The semaphore station was part of a line which at one time passed shipping advice at great speed from South Stack to Birkenhead and Liverpool.

*Puffin Island–Point Lynas*
Having passed the island, a course can be laid on Lynas Point, which is out of sight across the bay and about fifteen miles away. The first part of the leg is along the cliffs which show the outline of Arthur's Table. There is behind it a high radio mast, the red light of which can be seen above any low sea mist which may obscure the Trwyn Du light at the entrance to the Straits. Along the coastline of the bay there are small places to visit with shelter from the west to south west: Redwharf, Traeth Bychan, Moelfre and Dulas Bay.

*Redwharf Bay*   The name refers not to the whole bay (which dries) but to Red Wharf itself i.e. the old harbour of Port Llongdy beyond Shingle Point. The six mile passage from Puffin through Table Road is unremarkable except for Arthur's Table and above it the radio mast already mentioned. There is a clear entry mark (see photograph) on the prominent Castle Rock, with entry after four hours flood by the locally perched and buoyed channel; the line of moored boats can be seen under Castle Rock and followed in. There may be water to float at neaps in the Pool but in general all dries. The drill is to pick up or anchor and enquire at the Traeth Coch Clubhouse. The moorings here are really the only ones between Beaumaris and Holyhead, and feasible because there is shelter under the land round to about north, while the sands in the bay dry so high that they soon give cover from the easterly exposure. In emergency one can dry out behind Shingle Point, but this is no place for deep keel boats. Apart from the sailing club there are two pubs, but supplies are two miles distant.

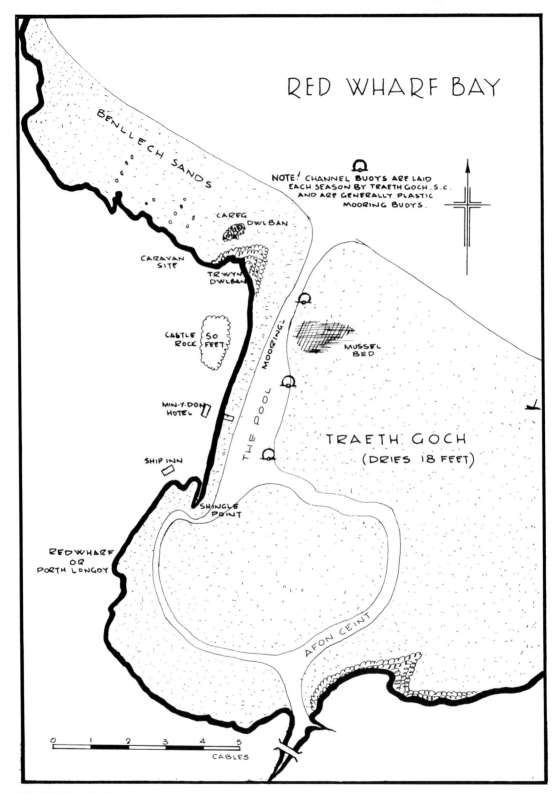

Fig. 17 Redwharf Bay.

102

*Redwharf Bay*. The key landmark of Castle Rock seen from the east. *Author*

*Moelfre Bay* Traeth Bychan is a charming little cove, drying half way out and naturally fully open to the north east, though sheltered from the west. One can anchor for the night in settled weather and the right forecast, and remain afloat or take the ground. The activity is dinghy sailing with a clubhouse and a cafe-shop-museum, with relics of the Royal Charter and the submarine *HMS Thetis*. Like Moelfre, the harbour is too open to allow permanent moorings.

*Moelfre* The charted advantages of Moelfre do not stand out on Chart No 1977, and the background story reads half the time of ships fleeing to shelter in Moelfre Roads or of them needing the services of the much chronicled Moelfre lifeboat. Good shelter or bad exposure is balanced on a knife edge. There is good shelter from gales from south, west and north, but the moment the wind veers through NE then it is necessary to find shelter in the Menai Straits. There is no harbour and no possibility of safe moorings, local boats being hauled up the shingle out of the water. Nevertheless it is possible to enjoy peace and comfort here while gales are roaring round Point Lynas and preventing further progress. If the wind is veering to the dangerous quarter, the swell coming in will give early warning of the need to move. Ynys Moelfre (or Rat Island) gives added protection and some old hands favour anchoring under its lee, but the Sound of Y Swint dries, and should not be used for passage.

From seaward the landmark is the newer lifeboat house, with red doors and a fixed amber light above the slip way, and the light on Moelfre Head. There is anchorage off the lifeboat slip but it is best to come right into the cove, dropping anchor off the old lifeboat house and using its slip for landing. The place to be

103

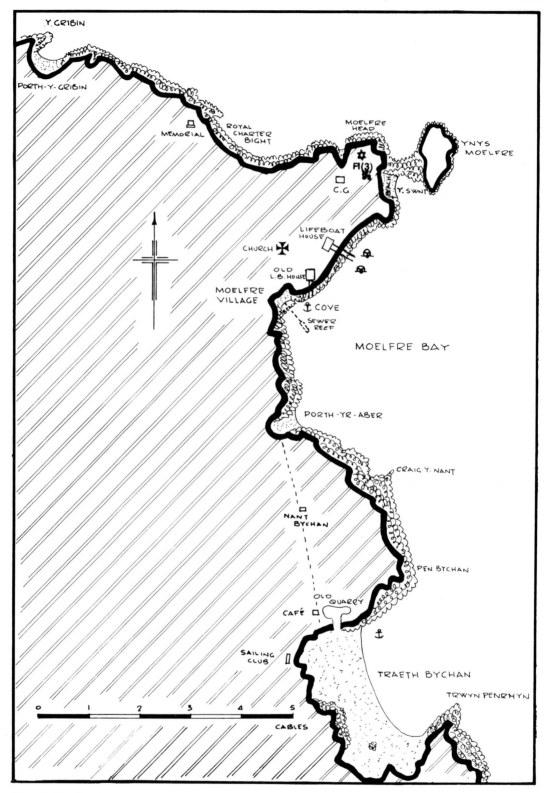

Fig. 18 Moelfre Bay.

104

avoided is the sewer outfall at the end of the sewer reef in the middle of the cove; this is unmarked but located by the quarrelling seabirds. The reef uncovers at springs and more than one yacht has been stranded there.

Ashore, the village is usually sheltered and warm with all supplies. There is an interesting cliff-top walk towards Lligwy Bay, showing the Royal Charter Bight and memorial. In the other direction it is possible to walk back across the fields to Traeth Bychan, where the shop and sailing club are open on Sundays whereas everything at Moelfre, including the pub, is closed.

### Point Lynas–Carmel Head

Leaving Moelfre Head astern, Lligwy and Dulas Bays are only for dinghy exploration. The course holds outside Ynys Dulas and its tower of refuge, and particularly away from the off-lier of Gareg Allan. Point Lynas may well be a point of decision. Going west one must carry the ebb and *vice versa*, and a westerly wind

*Lynas Point.* Seen from the south west. *Author*

may hamper or prevent traversing the north coast which is exposed without firm shelter. To Carmel Head is a passage of ten miles with no lit buoys. By night one is then forced to round into Holyhead Bay outside the Skerries lighthouse.

The definitive peninsula of Point Lynas, nearly a mile in length and headed due north, brings a ninety degrees change of course and wind. Heading now into westerly weather, this may prove too strong and suggest a return to Moelfre for shelter. The races can be circumvented by going outside, leaving the close inshore course for local talent. Immediately west of the head is the deep and gloomy Lynas Cove or Porth Eilean, which is suitable for anchorage and a short stay unless the wind decides to come straight in from the north. The old Point Lynas Lighthouse is the out-station for the Port of Liverpool (see photograph), is part of the Pilotage Service, and monitors the Offshore Oil Terminal. The Pilot Boat has been withdrawn and the ships lying waiting are serviced by launches from Amlych. Lynas is reputed to have a marine radiobeacon (PS) with a radius of 40 miles, but so far I have verified only the old 5 mile range. If on full range, the beacon would be a valuable lead-in from the Isle of Man, while the lee of Lynas itself is often a welcome break after a rough crossing.

*The Anglesey Offshore Oil Terminal*   This is now complete and operational, lying three miles off Amlych. At this range the very heavily moored yellow buoy appears small. It should not be closed by a yacht whose course will lie close in and crossing the pipeline, any anchoring being naturally banned; the buoy lighting is morse U, and so far there have been no reported problems in operation. Work and maintenance boats are based on Amlych. Yacht skippers need to be keenly aware of the terminal as they pass.

*Amlych*   Until the oil terminal this was a very decayed place previously used for the export of copper from Parys Mountain. It is still tidal from the old watch tower onwards, so that yachts can enter and dry out in complete shelter. It is not easily picked up from seaward, the landmarks being the chemical works (sight and smell of bromine fumes) and the island of East Mouse – pass either side.

Amlych has now been re-built to give a small outer harbour with water at all states behind a not-so-stout seawall. The entry is about fifty yards wide and comes in along the shore with a slate facing; unfortunately its axis is directly NE. In settled weather there is no difficulty, but the rare NE (or thereabouts) gale will sweep right in. Doing so will mean rebounding off the fronting wall and sweeping the outer wall and causing havoc. To a large extent this is reduced in the inner tidal harbour, but this needs water to enter. Its use as a refuge has therefore to be carefully calculated to avoid the trap. In normal times yachts are permitted to berth along the inner side of the outer wall, but the pens are for maintenance boats. The inner harbour has also been updated, and a drying out berth should not be difficult to find among the inshore fishing craft. The little town is half a mile away, but there are few amenities or services and to date no sailing club.

106

*Cemaes Bay*  From East Mouse island to Middle Mouse the coast is interesting from close in but offers no anchorage of note. Abeam of Middle Mouse is the three-quarter-mile wide entry to Cemaes Bay (pronounced Kemmis) opening fully to the NW, and thus the recipient of many a winter gale and some summer rolling swell. There is however good shelter from other angles and one can use fine tuning to find the best anchorage in a complex of small bays. It is an old and primitive harbour for small ships which were built here in times past. The dominant feature today is the atomic power station on Wylfa Head, the squat outline of which can be picked up many miles out to sea. It is of interest to yachtsmen really only in one particular: sometimes during a hot summer night it lets off high pressure superheated steam with a terrible roar, convincingly like an atomic explosion. Forewarned of this occasional possibility, one can get back into the bunk again.

Coming in at lowish water there is anchorage in settled weather in the middle of the bay or better under Fox Cliff to the east. With three or four hours flood there is enough water to go behind the breakwater and dry out; it is best to go ashore and negotiate this first (there is no Harbour Master, and arrangements are in the hands of a local boatowners association). Boats dry out and most of the harbour is quite

Fig. 19 Cemaes Bay.

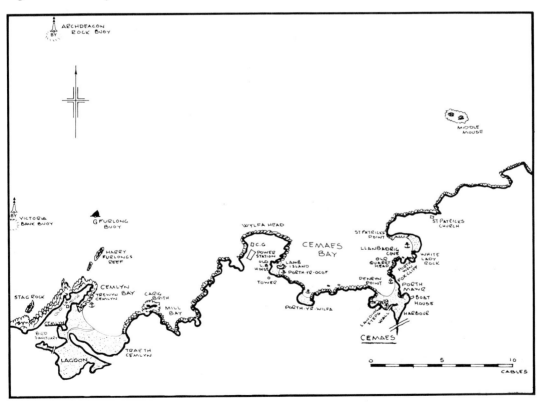

*Wylfa Head.* The dominating nuclear power station, visible many miles further to seaward than the Skerries lighthouse. *Author*

shallow and full of small boat moorings; there may be a swell and surge so that boats need watching down, while keel boats are not safe. Avoid landing on the beach if there is swell; there are steps at Port Bach.

There is a quiet and sheltered anchorage in Llanbadrig Cove round St Patrick Head, with a leading mark on the triangular White Lady Rock ashore; there are a few permanent moorings, and from here there are landing steps and a path to the village. Both lobster pots and scattered drying rocks are to be avoided. Lamb's Island is on the reciprocal side of the bay, giving westerly shelter under the power station. There are the old and historic lifeboat house together with the cave on the island; ashore is the observation tower and a path to the village which passes Porth-y-Wylfa.

Cruising people will be charmed with a stay in Cemaes which provides full supplies and a warm welcome. Easy weather is needed and when it begins to veer to the north it will be time to think about moving on across Holyhead Bay.

*Cemlyn Bay*   The contrast between Cemaes and Cemlyn is most striking, since they are separated only by Wylfa Head. Cemaes a lively cheerful family holiday village, while Cemlyn is a deserted solitary place, with hardly a house or a visitor, as if it had been cursed and shunned down its long history. A long history it certainly has, because it was mentioned by Pliny the Elder in AD 77 as being a source of salamander's wool or asbestos (Glazebrook). It is approached by grass grown lanes, where even the signposts have lost their pointing fingers. From seaward the mark is Harry's Furlong buoy, while the power station glooms to the east. It is possible to picture the little sailing coasters, infrequent as they were, offloading their coal and supplies and heading out as soon as possible. On entry from the west it is important never to pass inside the Furlong buoy.

One of the main factors in the unpopularity of Cemlyn must be that it is wide open to the NE gales, so dreaded on this part of the coast. The few light boats kept here are liable to be thrown ashore together with their moorings in such an event, and there is no sheltered part of the bay; in settled weather there is anchorage under the old and historic lifeboat house. The place is, however, a paradise for the birdwatcher, and the lagoon can be explored by dinghy. The fortress-like high walled structure on the west side is, in fact, a bird sanctuary built by a millionaire in the 1930's.

## Carmel Head–Holyhead

F H Glazebrook's 1936 *Inshore Passage* took this route round Carmel Head for the title of his pilot book, which was later to be published by *Yachting Monthly*, until about 1973, as *Anglesey and North Wales Coast Pilot*. A yacht rounds either close into the cliffs or well outside the Skerries. In my view the area between is No Man's Sea, full of sunken rocks, swirls, overfalls and races, through which a three to five knot stream surges and scours. Chart No 1413 nevertheless plots a big ship course on bearings which pass slap across the Langdon Ridge further into the bay, though avoiding the red sector of the Skerries light to the north. This is by no means a course to be advised for yachts, and indeed trawlers and coasters use the Inshore Passage where there is plenty of water close in, though a stream of 3½ to 5½ knots. There are, however, no lit marks inside the Skerries so that the passage is purely a daylight one.

Coming along from Cemaes Bay it is crucial to go outside Furlong buoy and inside both Victoria buoy and the beacon on West Mouse. At the White Lady beacons (onshore) the boat should be well in under the cliffs – lobster pots notwithstanding. With luck this leaves the rough water and races to seaward, in any case the affected area is short. Having used the Inshore Passage many times, on only one occasion has it been necessary to turn back with a north-easterly Force 5 over the flood, plus a timing error. It is thought locally that the flood begins to run at Carmel Head two hours before LW at Holyhead, which in any case is five miles away across the bay. Eastbound one needs to be at Carmel at the start of the flood to make the distance.

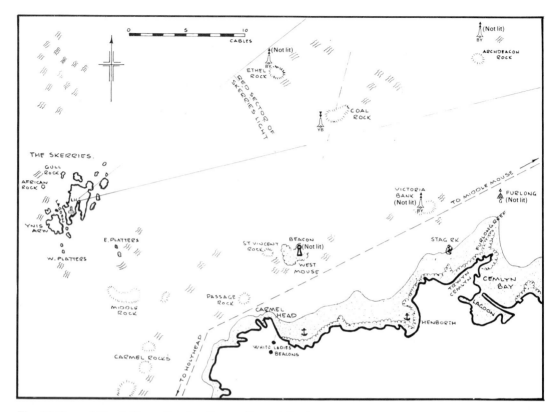

Fig. 20 Carmel Head. From Cemlyn Bay to Carmel Rocks.

*The Skerries*   These unpleasant rocks are charted to a larger scale on No 1413 rather than 1977, and have hosted one of the earliest and most profitable lighthouses in the business, before it was bought by Trinity House for a very large sum. From seaward it is low-lying and comes up much later than the Wylfa Head power station and Holy Mountain, the other marks for Holyhead Bay. If conditions are unsuitable to use the Inshore Passage and it is decided to pass outside the Skerries, a break-away from the shore should best leave the Middle Mouse to port. In view of the rough water likely to be met, it would be advisable to leave the three old ducks, Ethel, Coal and Archdeacon buoys, inshore; these are large and unlit and are indicated only by the red sector of the Skerries light. In order not to meet them at night, a wider course has to be juggled from the Lynas Point light, across the red sector, into the white sector and then down to the Skerries lighthouse. In rounding the Skerries one should keep well off, as it is an evil-looking lee shore.

*Holyhead Bay*   From Carmel Head to North Stack the chord of the Bay is six miles. Along this axis the streams run fast using the Skerries–Carmel gap, and make rough water over the Langdon Ridge. As a result it is often going to be difficult to lay and

110

*The Skerries.* An aerial view of the lighthouse, showing the Lagoon. *Author*

hold a course on the tip of the harbour breakwater; in any case the end of the breakwater should be given a good offing as rubble is tipped there. In westerly weather it is a great relief to win inside the great wall, especially when it can be seen that at the top-of-the-tide water may break clean over it.

*Holyhead Harbour*
Chart No 2011 is important as a full scale plan of the harbour layout, otherwise the situation will be confusing on first entry, particularly at night. It has to be clear that there are two harbours here, and the yachtsman does not use the Old Harbour. For centuries this was merely a muddy creek protected by Salt Island, but it has now been developed as a passenger and car ferry terminal with some commercial use.

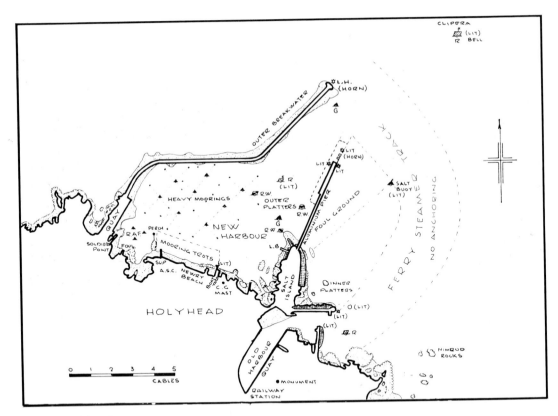

Fig. 21 Holyhead.

The New Harbour was designed as a much-needed Harbour of Refuge and the breakwater was started in 1847. The design is very much a railway conception and the twin of Dunleary – both harbours have a fatally large exposure to the NE though, in the case of Holyhead, an eastern arm was planned but not carried out. Such a breakwater would have been much in the same position as the present Aluminium jetty, which is however merely a pier and not of any real protection. The original plans can be seen in the sailing club.

The harbour entry is open between the charted black conical buoy and the Aluminium jetty. A course should be followed along the wall until its angle, then across to the mooring trots along Newry Beach. Visitors are asked to pick up a vacant mooring at the Mackenzie Landing end of the trots – the lighter moorings are inshore. There is no run in the harbour, and boats are wind rode with a rise and fall of just over 3½ metres (about twelve feet). The Holyhead SC and slip are at the head of the moorings by the Trinity House depot. There is a club boatman and a lunch service, with all supplies in the town and services at the boatyard.

Usually Holyhead is a sunny sheltered harbour and an active yachting centre, but if and when NE weather starts to come in, the picture is very much changed. It is a

112

*Holyhead.* Part of the inner harbour seen from the car ferry terminal. *Author*

time to see that the wire strop is lashed into the fairleads and a careful eye kept on the dinghy painter. It may be equally impossible to stay aboard or land at the slip, but luckily such occasions are rare if the forecasts are monitored. What is needed of course is the shelter of a marina, for which there is plenty of room at the top of the harbour. So far there have been no proposals for this.

As a transit port, Holyhead is noted for its communications rather than its attractions. There is a main line railway service and there will be a new road across Holy Island as part of the expressway. After one has walked the length of the breakwater and climbed to the top of Holy Mountain, there is little more in the way of local diversion.

### Holy Island

The largest scale chart is No 1413, which covers most of Holy Island, otherwise No 1977 is best. Round the prominent headlands of North Stack, South Stack and Penryn Mawr the stream runs up to five knots, but this rate falls quite rapidly as one moves further out to the more open sea. Wind and stream however can set up the Holyhead Race, so that one has to plan strategically to pass at the proper time in order to make a clean turn rather than a wide diversion. On the whole the ebb running against the prevalent south-westerly is the more troublesome, and it is interesting to see from the top of Holy Mountain that the races are very much in the pattern as set out in Chart No 1970. The mountain (about 200m or 700 ft) is the key

113

*Holy Island.* South Stack lighthouse seen from the south. *Author*

landmark when coming in from the west, but it may have a tablecloth, so that the S Stack Light is set lower at 60m or just under 200 ft. High and low water at S Stack is near enough to that of Holyhead itself so that, for our purposes, the best time to be there is HW slack in daylight. If making for Dublin Bay the same applies, but here it is best to keep away from North Stack and its race, taking a later back-bearing on S Stack, to gauge the N/S set of the stream.

It will have been noted that the station on North Stack is merely for a fog horn, and that behind Holy Mountain is a conspicuous radiomast – red lit; Gogarth Bay and Abraham's Bosom (!) are cliff-bound death traps. The overall cruising strategy will be to cover the twenty miles from Holyhead to Llanddwyn Island in one hop, bearing in mind that there is no convincing shelter en route on this exposed SW coast, nor any lights, though there is an easy stream. Caernarvon Bar can only be passed inwards on the flood, so that there will be some interesting navigational juggling to see how the whole passage to Caernarvon can be made non-stop in daylight. The reciprocal passage is much easier.

### The South-West Coast of Anglesey

Chart No 1970 covers this but is on a relatively small scale as there is little or no commercial or fishing traffic. Nor is there much cruising yacht activity in view of the prevalent onshore winds and the lack of good heavy weather shelter. Settled offshore weather is needed to exploit the rewards of the little places along the coast. For this Chart No 1970 is inadequate, making it difficult to name local coastline features. These are covered in detail with Sketch Maps in the *Anglesey Cruising Guide* to which local explorers must refer. Places covered include Trearddur Bay, Rhoscolyn, the Cymyran Strait, Rhosneigr, Aberffraw, and Maltraeth Bay. The RAF station at Aberffraw should be viewed with suspicion in view of the musketry and missile ranges – look for red flags. Coming down the coast, the two light towers on Llanddyn Island will probably show first, and it is then necessary to search further offshore to pick up the rather small can and cone fairway buoys of the Caernarvon Bar; their siting is variable as they are moved to conform with shifting banks.

It might be noted that Chart No 1970 shows the Bar to be sited in the NE corner of Caernarvon Bay, being fully open from the west and SW, and having a long and tricky entry. When such winds rate higher than Force 5, the Bar may be impassable, particularly on the ebb but also on the flood. It is thus inadvisable to come creaming in from the west if this is a possibility, and much wiser to divert early to Holyhead.

*Llanddwyn Island* Chart No 1464 shows that the two approach buoys have now been altered to IALA pattern. The functioning lighthouse tower is that on the South Prong near Pilots' Cove, which is so named because it was a pilot station in the days of the busy slate trade; there is now almost no commercial traffic and the pilot is at Caernarvon. Pilots' Cove and, to a lesser degree, Mermaid Cove, are cruising gems, but in addition there is anchorage sheltered from west and north, and there are good beaches for drying out. Here one can wait for the tide or for the bar to settle, or spend a comfortable night. On strong easterlies the place is fairly explosed.

Llanddwyn is only an island at high spring tides, but it is cut off from civilisation by having only a jeepable track. The excisemen laid a group of drug smugglers by the heels when they used Pilot's Cove in the early eighties. Like so many remote islands it was in former times a place of saintly pilgrimage, showing the ruins of an abbey, crosses and a magic wishing well; beyond a well there are no yachting amenities. At this stage it is not proposed to cross Caernarvon Bar, but to return to the NE entrance to the Menai Strait and describe its passage.

Pilot's Cove. *Sarahay* in a snug anchorage at low water. *Author*

### The Menai Strait or Straits

Chart No 1464, with inset plan of the Swellies, most faithfully reports every detail of the topography. As a result it merits the most careful study by cruising skippers, since all is by no means plain sailing. In my *Anglesey Cruising Guide* the account and the sketch maps are on a more sophisticated scale than can be attempted here. The twenty miles of fairly protected water is reputed to be the jewel in the crown of Irish Sea cruising. It runs NE to SW from Puffin Island to Aber Menai and then out to the Caernarvon fairway buoys. It is certainly no tidal backwater, having a high rise and fall and strong streams of a complex nature. The bottleneck of the Swellies has a spring stream of up to eight knots and its passage has to be carefully worked out. The tidal rise at the NE end in Liverpool Bay is nine feet higher than at the SW end in Caernarvon Bay, where the flood starts earlier; so that the tides work every which-way and the stated HW times are to be ignored. Nevertheless the Swellies can be perfectly safely passed by yachts providing the timing is exactly right; if this is so then one can row through in a dinghy. At the wrong time the Swellies are a wrecker

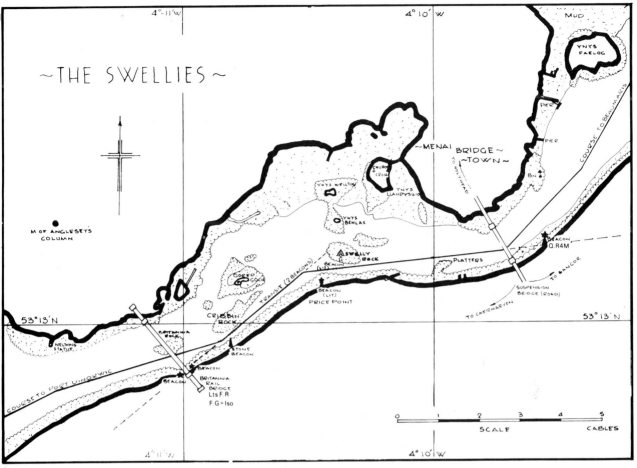

Fig. 22 The Swellies. From Britannia Rock to Ynys Faelog.

of boats. There was some criticism of my over-cautious views of this hot sound in the first edition, and indeed one could see more than the occasional boat coming through in a slap-happy manner. Last season I had the opportunity of seeing a group of twelve yachts coming through. They waited below the railway bridge and then came through in a convoy at exactly the right time. The inevitable late-comer was caught by the sudden turn of the tide and had to withdraw. On this occasion there was an inflatable rescue boat on duty, the only 'natural' for such a habitat.

## The Beaumaris Channel

This four-mile stretch is used extensively by yachts and small craft, but has almost no commercial traffic at present. The only hazard is that of running aground on either hand on a falling tide, or of venturing to cross the great area of drying sandbanks which look so tempting when covered. The buoyage is the minimum that could be devised and a double buoyed route has long been needed. The elusive buoy is B 8. At Penmon Point the extra buoy marks a wreck. Just north of the wreck buoy there is anchorage with fair westerly shelter, from which a visit can be made to Penmon Priory. By daylight the course is simple enough provided that the buoys are carefully checked. On the other hand, a night passage calls for

117

Caernarvon 6 M
SW
Anglesey
Leading marks
Cribbin Rk
Gored Coch
Price's beacon (replaced)
Mainland
Swellies Rk and new beacon
Britannia Rk
The Platters
Telford's bridge
NE

*The Swellies.* Looking SW from Beaumaris Channel, with the suspension bridge in the foreground.
*Author*

considerable experience as some of the essential buoys are unlit or non-existent. (This is also true of the rest of the Straits. Indeed with the loss of the Swelly Rock light, it is doubtful whether a licensed pilot could safely take a ship through in the dark.) The actual lighting of the Beaumaris Channel is shown in the sketch map taken from the *Anglesey Cruising Guide*. But even so, those who have a permanent mooring at Beaumaris or beyond find a night return a nail-biting exercise.

*Beaumaris*
Though this is the main centre of the Straits yachting activity, it is no harbour but merely a very narrow part of the channel with shelter from west to north. The north-going flood, with its earlier start, threads the Swellies and passes Beaumaris before meeting the south-going flood. The tidesmeet is then gradually forced back until some sort of stability is reached at Bangor Pool. There the superior height of the south-going stream wins and sweeps through the Swellies as the ebb. Thus at Beaumaris the streams are confusing, and usually strong enough to make dinghy work dangerous – specially at night. The narrowness of the channel at this point

118

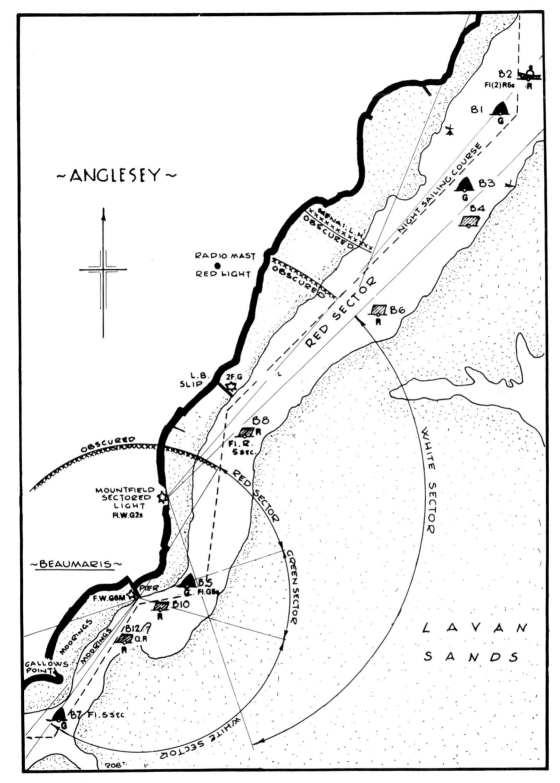

Fig. 23 Beaumaris Channel. North east from Gallows Point.

adds its problem. So that though with luck it may be possible to sail in and pick up a mooring, alternatives have to be considered: the Royal Anglesey YC have visitors' moorings and a boatman, which may solve the problem, but the following advice may be given otherwise.

1. Do not try to anchor between the Pier and Gallows Point as the bottom is littered with old moorings. Drop anchor either soon after passing B 5 or behind Gallows Point beyond B 7. The Pool offshore of B 10 is another possibility.

2. Inside buoys B 10 and 12 is the channel, and outside them is a steep bank which is a popular and very public place to run aground on the ebb.

3. Inside the deep water moorings the tidal moorings dry to inaccessible mud. There is landing at the boatyard, the pier or the beach, and there are full services and supplies.

There can be little more pleasant than to lie at Beaumaris looking at the panoramic views of the sun on Snowdonia. The town is drenched in history with the emphasis on punishment if not crime. There are old inns, a castle, a Dickensian assize court, and a prison, while the hangman had his gibbet on Gallows Point.

*Beaumaris*. An attractive facade from the water. *Author*

## Gallows Point to Menai Bridge

Menai Bridge is both the name of the small township which grew up as the bridge was building between 1819 and 1826, and the suspension bridge itself. On the Anglesey shore there are private moorings, though none on the mainland shore where most of the stream runs. In Bangor Pool are seven big-ship mooring buoys, which are far too heavy for yachts to use. Further on are another three heavy moorings to which lie three concrete barges of World War I vintage; casual berthing alongside is forbidden by notice, but on occasion one is forced by some nautical exigency or other to do this, the result being a comfortable night and an inspiring view of the bridge. The new floating stage at Menai bridge is both expensive and limited in berths, but otherwise the exact place to wait for the Swellies passage. Anchoring is not a good policy but there may be a vacant mooring. While waiting it is instructive to take a look at the run of the Swellies either from the bridge or the Anglesey bank. The ebb runs for seven and a half hours, and at low water the rocky hazards stand out well. Menai Bridge is a pleasant little town, well supplied with pubs as a relic of the former pleasure steamers.

Fig. 24 Bangor.

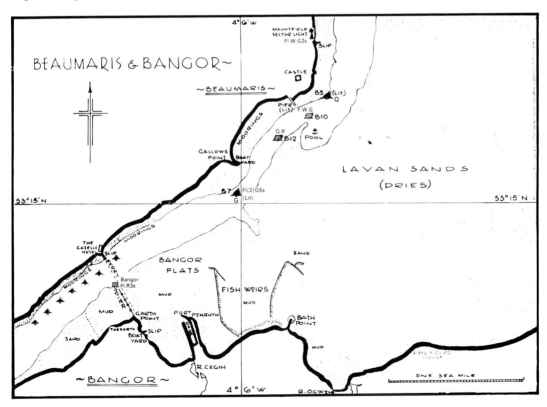

## Bangor

The sketch map taken from my *Anglesey Cruising Guide* shows the topography. Opposite the New Bangor pier (now condemned and disused) lies the Gazelle Inn, a focal yachting centre with fair shelter. There is no boatman or sailing club but many moorings stretch away towards Gallows Point and there are usually vacancies. From here it is possible to row across to the Garth where there are shops. Bangor is silted up, there is rather exposed anchorage on the edge of the bank round the pier head, while Dickies' boatyard and slips are on the Garth.

## Port Penrhyn

This little-known and little-used old slate harbour is a magnificently fully sheltered bolt-hole for those occasions when gales from the SW (or NE) scour through the Straits. It is tidal but used by trawlers, having about ten feet of water at the entry on HW. The approach across the flats can be seen on the chart as about a quarter of a mile NE of Bangor pier, with marker poles at the entrance. Once in, the Harbour Master will advise about a berth, the bottom being level mud. Ladders are scanty, but the boat will be afloat in good time to calculate the Swellies passage. The town

*Port Penrhyn.* A spacious, well-protected tidal harbour. *Author*

122

the Garth and the boatyard and chandlery, are within easy walking distance. It has now been proposed that the area between the Garth and Port Penrhyn should become a marina.

## The Swellies

It has to be admitted that the hazards depicted in the plan in Chart No 1464 are fearsome, the more so when it is realised that for most of the time a five to eight knot stream is running at a constant maximum. The sketch map simplifies the picture and shows the only possible course to be taken – close into the mainland bank. However, like other high rate sounds, this one is innocuous at slack water when its mile length can be passed in a dinghy. The Swellies slack lasts for twenty minutes at springs and forty minutes at neaps, with a rapid build-up to maximum after reversal. On one occasion at low water neaps I took *Sarahay* in under the Suspension Bridge, went down to the Tubular Bridge and then returned without the slightest trouble. Otherwise I know from another personal experience in another boat that nothing less than ten knots of speed is needed to creep against the ebb. The marks are scanty, beacons are needed on the Platters and the Cribbin Rock, while the replacement of the Swellie Rock beacon by a buoy can be misleading.

*The Swellies.* Looking NW over Cribbin Rock and Gored Coch. The passage shown by the arrow is going north-east, and lies between the mainland (off the bottom of the picture) and Cribbin Rock, showing at half-ebb. *Author*

123

As to the timing of slack water one feels that there should be a large notice slung from the arch of the Suspension Bridge: *High Water Slack is Two Hours Before HW Liverpool.* Low water slack is more elastic, as the ebb runs up to seven and a half hours. The preferred time to pass either way is at HW in daylight. At LW springs it is possible to touch near the railway bridge, while in the passage to and from Caernarvon there will be an adverse stream. In passing towards Beaumaris it is reasonably safe, though rather speedy, to go after four hours flood; before this time it is dangerous. To be swept through on the ebb is always too dangerous even on neaps. With the loss of the Swellie Rock beacon stranding on the rock has become popular, but there are helicopters at Valley Airfield.

There is only one safe course to follow, shown in the sketch map attached. From the Beaumaris direction at HW slack it is as follows:

1. Locate the back beacon on the mainland side above the suspension bridge, and pass under the centre of the arch, leaving the Swellie Rock buoy to starboard.
2. Alter to Price's beacon on the mainland, until the lit transit marks under the railway bridge are in line.
3. Follow the transit line until the triangular stone beacon on the mainland side. Then alter to starboard to pass under the bridge.

The old tubular railway bridge has, after a fire in recent years, been replaced by a graceful arch which also carries a four-lane road crossing. There is still the hundred feet clearance as demanded by the Navy for their first raters in the early 19th century, though the loss of *HMS Conway* showed that the passage was impossible for the deep-drafted old sailing ships. Smaller yachts should note that they will usually be prevented from sailing through because the prevailing wind will be ahead or blanketed by the high ground, and that there is no safe room for tacking. A strong reliable engine is needed, with a reverse gear; the latter because, if caught on the wrong foot, it is unwise to attempt to turn the boat, whereas when caught in the ebb, going astern on the engine may give better control. The important thing is not to make any mistakes on spring tides.

### The South West Menai Straits

Chart No 1464 shows that the eight-mile stretch from the Swellies to Aber Menai has important differences from the NE section. It is isolated to some extent by the timing of the Swellies at one end and the troublesome Caernarvon Bar at the other; the prevalent south-westerlies sweep though without much shelter; there is a conventional ebb and flow, but at each end there is a spring stream of five knots; predicted HW times are correct, and the tidal levels (see table in chart) are six to nine feet below the rises for the NE arm; the SW exit is narrow and deep because of a remarkable sand dune spit – the South Crook (this doesn't directly concern yachtsmen but it is fascinating to speculate how and why it has been set up and maintained).

The buoyage calls for particular alertness on the part of the skipper/navigator because of a built-in trap. From Puffin to Caernarvon the numbering of buoys is in sequence, the additional lettering changing from B to C after the Swellies, as the Caernarvon Harbour Trustees take over. The pillar buoy off Caernarvon marks the Head of Navigation, after which the cones and the cans most disconcertingly change sides, so that it is all too easy to pass on the wrong side and run aground. Coming in from seaward the siding is conventional up to Caernarvon. The change-over is now more clearly shown on the chart by confronting direction of buoyage arrows. The executive buoy is now a south cardinal (pillar) and is charted 'change'.


*Port Dinorwic*

After leaving the Brittania railway bridge there is a sense of anticlimax as one passes into a river-like channel. Plas Newydd shows a pleasing frontage, which was designed by James Wyatt, as was the Harbour Office at Port Penrhyn. Dinorwic has both an old and a new image. As an active centre of the slate trade its small locally-built sailing ships took their cargoes far and wide – even round the Horn. The slate trade failed in the early years of this century, and since then the place has been a gloomy ghost town. More recently an attempt was made to set up a marina project, but this is now in liquidation with nothing built. The only tangible result is mooring trots between two lit and charted buoys off the housing development; these are uncomfortable and exposed to the strong stream.

The Vaynol Dock has survived from the slate days. This has a manned entry lock with so-called marina berthing inside. These are good permanent berths, but not of interest for cruising boats, though Snowdonia is close inland. The tidal dock is silted but it may be entered at HW. There are privately laid moorings along the mainland side, at Moel-y-Don and beyond Dinas where anchorage is fairly clear; vacancies may not be very reliable. The stream runs hard through Dinorwic, and when this is against weather from the SW it may not be possible to land. There are supplies ashore (the Welsh lamb is particularly good), a sailing club, and a chandlery store.


*Foel Ferry*

The Barras Channel does not show well on the chart, but it opens at C 11 buoy as a continuation of the secondary channel along the Anglesey shore. The ferry still functions in the summer round HW using the Swatchway, but this is not suitable for yachts. If entering the Barras on the ebb, care is needed, for the remains of the low tide jetty are still under the water. There is anchorage in the pool and landing at the high tide jetty with only light boat moorings. The Mermaid Inn is not always in commission and there are only scattered houses ashore. This is a sheltered and remote anchorage – perhaps even sinister. On the main channel side of the high drying Traeth Gwyllt, there can be very rough water when the strong young flood is running in a narrow channel against a strong wind. A similar situation may be found towards the end of the ebb.

125

*Caernarvon*. At low water. The swing bridge across the entry channel is open, and the slate quay is hidden behind the main castle buildings. *Author*

## Caernarvon

This is a busy market and tourist town with the site of the Roman town of Segontium just inland. The superb approach vista of the castle has survived unchanged since it was completed by Edward I seven hundred years ago. From its topmost tower there is an all-embracing view of the bar and estuary. In the days of sail, Caernarvon was crowded with ships loading at the Slate Quay or in the large tidal dock. Though both dry, there is good shelter and the harbour is full of yachts and other small boats. The dock is neither gated nor locked and has not yet been turned into a marina. There is plenty of space for this to be done but underlying rock would make the operation costly.

Entry to Caernarvon is at C9 – note that the Head of Navigation buoy has now been passed and the direction of buoyage has already changed. After turning the Fairway buoy, the channel continues across the front of the castle with four small floats to starboard (uncharted). The swing bridge is manned when there is water, and it is left open at night. As the harbour is crowded the best ploy is to tie up temporally outside a boat at the Slate Quay and see the Harbour Master. The bottom is level and fairly clean but anchoring would be unwise. Only the trickle of

126

the River Seiont remains at LW, and keel boats may fall outwards. If a berth is obtained, then the boat is in a bright sunny harbour in the centre of the town. The river is not navigable for any useful distance and the quays above the Slate Quay are privately owned. Opposite the quay there is shelving beach suitable for laying-up, together with a small boatyard. The swing bridge is pedestrian and leads only to the baths and foreshore.

It is possible to lie at anchor fairly comfortably off the dock, away from the fairway to the harbour and out of the stream in the channel. The dock can also be used by yachts, though it is by no means picturesque and dries to deep mud; there are slipways but few ladders, but it is convenient for the town. Caernarvon itself is rather a self-contained town with no railway link, but Snowdonia lies close inland. There are two clubs ashore, the Royal Welch YC and the Caernarvon SC, both of which offer hospitality to visitors. The castle is of great historical interest.

# XI   Cardigan Bay

## Charts

| No | Title | Scale 1: |
|----|-------|----------|
| 1464 | Menai Strait. | 25,000 |
|  | The Swellies. | 10,000 |
| 1478 | St Govan's Head to St David's Head. | 75,000 |
| 1482 | Plans on the coast of south-west Wales: | — |
|  | Tenby and Saundersfoot with approaches. | 25,000 |
|  | Ramsey Sound, with the Bishops and Clerks. | 25,000 |
|  | Jack Sound. | 12,000 |
| 1484 | Plans in Cardigan Bay: | — |
|  | Fishguard Bay; New Quay. | 12,500 |
|  | Aberystwyth; St Tudwal's roads. | 18,000 |
|  | Aberdovey; Barmouth. | 25,000 |
|  | Aberporth. | 30,000 |
|  | Approaches to Cardigan. | 37,500 |
| 1970 | Caernarvon Bay. | 75,000 |
| 1971 | Cardigan Bay – northern part. | 75,000 |
| 1972 | Cardigan Bay – central part. | 75,000 |
| 1973 | Cardigan Bay – southern part. | 75,000 |
| 2878 | Approaches to Milford Haven. | 25,000 |

## The Caernarvon Channel

As shown in Chart No 1464, the two-mile stretch between the town and Aber Menai is straightforward enough, provided that the direction of buoyage is clearly in mind. The actual entry/exit is narrow, three to four hundred yards wide and fifty feet deep. The constriction is due to the two claw-like sandspits of South Crook and Morfa Dinlleu, behind which are the mile wide flats of Traeth Melynog and Foryd Bay. In the Narrows the stream runs roughly six hours in either direction, turning with about half an hour's difference from Holyhead. In the charted stream table the flood would seem to be the faster, but in the admiralty Pilot the rate is said to be five knots in both directions at springs and mid-tide; a trawler could better these figures but not many yachts. Thus there is a tide gate here, less heavily sprung of course at neaps. Bearing in mind the shallows of the Bar, the outward passage may be made only in the first four hours of the ebb and the inward passage in the last four hours of the flood.

There are waiting places on the outside at Pilots' Cove, and just above the Mussel Bank buoy, on the inside behind Belan, and on the north side at what might be called Crook Haven behind Aber Menai Point; in the last two places there is a constant back-eddy, and boats hunt round their anchors all night. Crook Haven is a popular yacht resort and there are some permanent moorings but nothing ashore. At HW the South Crook is only a narrow strip of sand, but it holds off the seas if not the SW winds. Fort Belan is a period piece built during the Napoleonic wars to defend the entrance. Recently I heard one of its pieces fire and the ball passed neatly through the mainsail of a passing yacht.

*Caernarvon Bar*

In Chart No 1464 the three-mile entrance channel is buoyed reasonably well, but the banks shift after SW gales and the buoys have to be moved; not all are lit and a night entry is not advised for first timers, there being little or no commercial traffic. The pilot is at Caernarvon, and it is best to check the chart before leaving. In general, westerlies above Force 4 or 5 make the bar dangerous for yachts (and

Fig. 25 Caernarvon Bar.

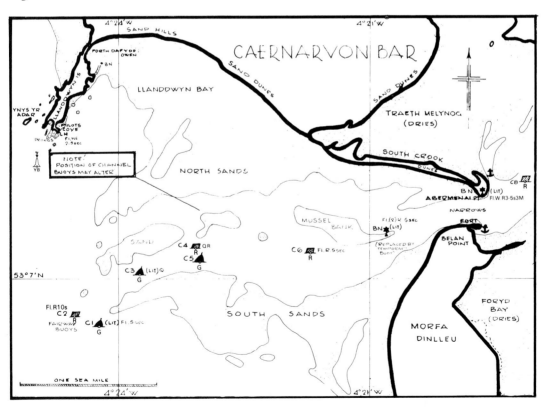

deadly for the old sailing ships), so that it can be passed only with the stream, the last four hours of the flood and the first four of the ebb. Inward there is shelter at Pilots' Cove (dealt with earlier) or anchorage at a pinch off the Mussel Bank, but once committed it is going to be difficult to turn back. It is important not to be trapped into this NE angle of Caernarvon Bay only to be faced with an impassable bar. The fairway buoys are small and not easy to find, as well as being very mobile. On leaving on the ebb it is not going to be possible to head back against the stream. In such a case one is forced to anchor off the Mussel Bank, with wind over tide kicking up a rough sea.

The topography of the bar is that of a delta set up by the fierce scour of the ebb out of the Straits. Initially, as far as the Mussel Bank (the old Beacon has been swept away), the channel is deep; Further out the sandbanks begin to appear and there is no clear main channel. Bearing in mind that the boat will be going out on the ebb, it is not a place at which to hang about as the level drops. Local yachtsmen will be seen to cross the South Bank but there are no marks, and strangers must stick to the buoys until near to C1 and C2. I have not personally experienced any excitement in crossing Caernarvon Bar, but there is plenty of evidence of its problems.

### Caernarvon Bay

Charts Nos 1970 and 1971 are both rather small scale, but then there is little serious sea traffic. In general terms both Caernarvon and Cardigan Bay are inhospitable for yachtsmen due to prevalent onshore winds and poor harbours. A skipper might well be forgiven if he decided to head straight for Fishguard or Milford Haven, outside everything but the Smalls. To explore the coastline, settled easterly weather, such as is likely early in the season, is called for. Running down the Lleyn Peninsula, the Rivals stand out magnificently, but there is little comfort except possibly at Port Trevor, where there is a drying stone jetty.

### *Porth Dinllaen*

The shelter here is given by a freak peninsula, three quarters of a mile in length, heading directly north. When the wind veers past this point, heavy swell comes in on a long fetch and it will be necessary to look for better shelter, for instance at Pilots' Cove which is upwind. As a result it has never been developed and is not used by fishing boats, while yachts are at constant risk from NE gales. There are however some moorings jealously guarded and of variable reliability. Anchorage is possible rather further out and there is the reassurance of the lifeboat; visitors may be able to negotiate the temporary use of its standby mooring. In settled weather from the sheltered arcs it is a pleasant place for a short stay and there is good fishing in the bay. Ashore there is a good pub with a six-day licence. Connection with Morfa Nevin is by track. It is a useful place to wait for the timing through Bardsey Sound.

130

*Bardsey Sound*

Chart No 1971 is over-reassuring, while the information in the Admiralty Pilot is not easy for the amateur in a small boat to interpret. Though Bardsey Island is heavily noted for rips and overfalls all round, the Sound itself is deceptively clear of these markings. The Sound is wide at one and a half miles across, and free of hazards except for Carreg Dhu inshore. It would seem then invitingly simple to round from Braich-y-Pwll to Pen-y-cil, were it not for the stream arrow showing 5 to 6 knots through the Sound (the rates fall to more normal figures in surrounding areas). HW times at Bardsey Island are three hours in advance of Liverpool and the stream runs roughly six hours in either direction. To detour round Bardsey calls for a wide sweep and avoidance of both Bastram Shoal and the Devil's Ridge, a much longer passage.

It is a basic necessity, therefore, to pass through the Sound with the stream, waiting if necessary in Porth Dinlaen or Aberdaron. With settled weather, in my experience this is simple enough but not a night exercise since the shore is quite unlit. However Bardsey Sound has a thoroughly deserved bad reputation, dependent not only on the rate of flow of the stream but also on the force and direction of the wind. Even with a favourable flow, winds above Force 5 (either ahead of astern) will give a wickedly disturbed sea. The classic situation is being pushed into the Sound by a strong north-westerly or a south-westerly, and then being held there by an opposing stream; Hilaire Belloc in *The Cruise of the Nona* has left a wonderful word picture of just this. From a personal experience, due to poor judgement and bad timing, it was possible to confirm his account in every detail. After half an hour of ardent prayer, and with the help her powerful engine, *Sarahay* pulled herself clear but neither before nor since has she been so knocked about. Oddly enough, the respect due to Bardsey Sound is either not mentioned or hardly mentioned in the various publications and almanacs available, though it must be much used by yachts from both Abersoch and Pwllheli.

## Cardigan Bay

Having passed through Bardsey Sound, hopefully with good judgement, Pen-y-cil is rounded and Aberdaron's gloomy bay opens. Being fully open to the prevalent south-westerlies, there are no moorings, and the swell cannot be avoided even by trying for shelter behind the small islands. Anchorage is immediately off the small village, and landing on the beach is often through the surf which may upset the dinghy; Port Meudy under the cliffs may be a safer landing. The bay is perhaps good for a night stop-over with a good forecast; supplies are meagre and there is no sailing club. The significance of Aberdaron is mainly historical, as it was and is the traditional access point for Bardsey Island. In centuries past many pilgrimages were made to this island of saints, which is now a bird sanctuary. It is always difficult to make the passage across the Sound and, while waiting for suitable weather, the pilgrims roistered in the inns of Aberdaron, which luckily are still in existence,

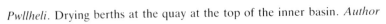

Buoyed channel
←
entry to port

Lit sewer beacon
—leave well to
port

*Pwllheli.* The lit sewer beacon on the approach should be left well to port. *Author*

*Pwllheli.* Drying berths at the quay at the top of the inner basin. *Author*

Beyond Aberdaron is the well named Hell's Mouth to be crossed before coming into St Tudwall's Roads.

*Abersoch*

In sailing ship days the islands gave some shelter from the south and a good lee from both west and south, while the very small drying harbour of Abersoch was secure. Today's large sailing activity is based on several hundred moorings, stretching out in fairly shallow water from the South Caernarvonshire YC. Here the shelter is not so good, as heavy ground tackle and high insurance rates show. Gales from the easterly arc prove very damaging, and the visitor living aboard will find the rolling troublesome. There is bound to be a vacant mooring, and its temporary use can be discussed with the boatman. The launch service is excellent, with a slip and hospitable clubhouse ashore. Supplies in the village are good, while in addition there is a boatyard and chandlery. There is a pleasant ambience at Abersoch as one sits watching the racing in smooth offshore weather, but the forecasts have to be carefully watched as full shelter is scarce hereabouts.

If the swell on the moorings becomes troublesome, then it may well be possible to get a good night's sleep by drying out. This is best done in the west part of the bay, either by the old lifeboat house or closer in. Entrance to the harbour can only be made across the sands at HW to enter the mouth of the Afon Soch; exit will be equally restricted. Though Abersoch offers deep water mooring or anchorage, to enjoy it from the cruising angle calls for settled weather offshore. In the absence of this one needs a stable living room floor ashore.

*Pwllheli*

This harbour has a great natural advantage in that the Morfa Gareg curves round the entrance to head north and there is only a limited exposure from this arc. The slate traders used a large inner harbour, but the two rivers entering and lack of dredging have resulted in it silting up. Approach is made easy by conspicuous tall boarding houses of Victorian vintage. In good weather there is anchorage off the Morfa in deep water with cover from the north; this may be an advantage, for the moorings in the channel are crowded and dry out. The entrance is buoyed from the fairway to guide round the spit, which only begins to cover at half flood. There can be no anchoring, and visitors can make enquiries as to a council-laid mooring at the sailing club; at low water there may well be the usual problem of getting ashore. Moorings fill the whole channel inside the last buoy, centring on the Pool which may retain some water at LWS. Recently trot chains were introduced on the north bank of the channel, and the south bank is due to be treated in a similar manner; this should lead to a much more economical use of the space.

It can be seen that Pwllheli is an active though crowded yachting centre, but on this awkward coast and throughout Cardigan Bay it is crucial when cruising: with the prevalent on-shore winds, it may be the only place which is safely accessible between

*Portmadoc*. Berthing is either along the quay, or else in mid-stream. *Author*

*Portmadoc*. Drying berths in the inner harbour. *Author*

Holyhead and Fishguard. To be sure it has a bar, but unlike the other harbours it faces north and not west. A marina has been proposed at Pwllheli on many occasions without coming to fruition; presumably this would mean the gating and dredging of the inner harbour which is walled or quayed round. As can be seen from the photograph, quite large boats can reach the top wall, but only on HW and exit is restricted to this. Cruising boats should enquire about the possibilities of a completely sheltered berth here. The latest news is that the current plan for a marina is going ahead, it is the only possible answer to the overcrowding.

## Portmadoc

The fairway buoy is charted on No 1971, but not the channel buoys because they have to be moved frequently. It is doubtful whether any of the channel buoys are lit, while the fairway, though lit, is hard to spot in the daylight. There is a significant bar, at its worst when there is an onshore wind over the ebb, so that entry may be impossible. The tricky entrance did not deter the previously prosperous and enterprising slate trade seeking a secure port. The slate was originally brought down from the hills by river boats, later by horse-drawn trains and steam trains, and the line across Mr Maddock's embankment is now active again. Some of the earliest steam tugs were used to overcome the difficulties of the channel. At one time there was active ship building, but today there is no ship or trawler traffic. In more recent time the harbour has been bought from the Tremadoc Estate by the town council and a Harbour Master has rationalised the mooring situation, which was rather chaotic with several interests involved.

Provided then that the bar is friendly, it can be passed by the visitor after half flood – it is almost dry after half ebb, and the channel is nearly four miles in length. On reaching the point of Ynys Cyngar, the channel holds under the land past Borth-y-Gest leaving Lewis Island to starboard. Here the shore is quayed and is the site of a boat yard. It might be best to tie up here and make enquiries from the Harbour Master as to a more permanent berth. There may be room to go to the top of the harbour and tie outside one of the boats there. The harbour is well sheltered – Lewis Island being artificially formed from the ballast of incoming trading vessels. There is a great deal of yachting activity and a sailing club, while the town provides all supplies. There is much of interest ashore that would repay a few days' stay, though this may be forcibly prolonged if the weather from the west sets in strong.

## Mochras Lagoon (Shell Island)

Chart No 1971 gives a fair idea of the unusual entrance. This lies two miles south of Harlech Castle and will call for a search, as there is no fairway buoy. It is a terminal coastal lagoon for the Afon Artro, breaking through the sandhills and underlying rock to reach the sea. For the stranger the entrance may prove impossible with onshore winds, but it may serve its turn as there is complete shelter inside, though it is isolated with no amenities. The problem is to locate the entrance as the sheltering

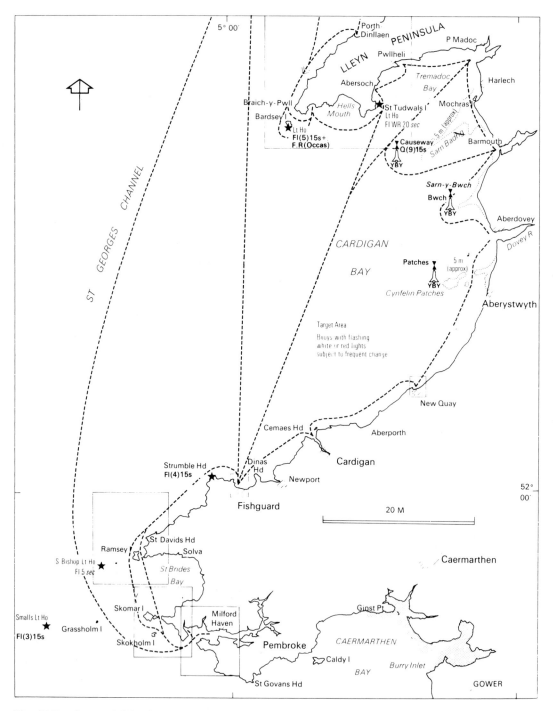

Fig. 26 Bardsey to Milford Haven. Cardigan Bay.

sandbanks overlap from seaward, and one has to double behind the spit. Having gained the channel it initially runs south, then turns through a rightangle to run into the lagoon; to port there is an old sea wall and the channel is marked with red posts. Inside there is no chart-work except that of the channel in the river bed. There are private moorings here with a track running down from the village of Llanbedre. The fairway, which dries, runs by the northern side and at HW can be taken to reach the quay at the railway crossing; this is a very snug berth. The whole topography makes an interesting exploration.

*St Patrick's Causeway (Sarn Badrig)* If we are to continue to Barmouth it is necessary to negotiate in some way this extraordinary and dangerous sunken causeway, forming the southern boundary of Tremadoc Bay. If coming from Bardsey, Aberdaron, Abersoch or Pwllheli, the course would naturally be laid outside the Causeway buoy and a very sincere effort would be made to locate it. This is the only buoy defining the hazard and it lies at the tip of its twelve-mile stretch. Oddly enough very little attempt has been made to explore or record this feature, which must have been a terrible trap for the old sailing ships and no less for yachts. It must be significant that a historic wreck has been declared in the angle which the Sarn makes with the coast. Only parts emerge at LAT, so that in the upper reaches of the tide it would in calm weather be open for exploration. If this has been done there is nothing on record, and Frank Cowper reported this and similar formations to be crumbling and sinking.

That the east passage should exist is another oddity. This allows a boat to round the landward end of the Sarn in an unexpected way. Though the passage has no marks or buoys, the chart shows water at all states and plenty at half tide. Starting from Mochras Point and using the echo sounder as a blindman's stick, the channel runs between half and a quarter mile off-shore. When the shallowing of the Bemar Bank begins to register, the yacht can be conned away from the coast before heading for Barmouth; it is however a passage to be taken only in fair weather. It may be that the seaward red section of the St Tudwal lighthouse, seven miles away, may be intended to warn against crossing the outer end of the Sarn should the warning buoy not light up. Both Frank Cowper and the Admiralty Pilot give detailed instructions for passing the east passage, but to me these are confusing and moreover dependent on recognisable distant landmarks being in the clear.

*Barmouth*
There is a port plan in Chart No 1484. Having entered Cardigan Bay this harbour is typical of those that will be met when moving south. Facing west into the prevalent wind, there is a bar to be crossed and entrance is to a coastal lagoon between sand spits. With strong onshore winds nearly all these harbours will be denied to the visiting stranger, who will need settled easterly weather to explore them. At Barmouth there is easy location by the Outer Fairway buoy from which the channel buoys can be seen ahead. To the south the channel is bounded by the long

rock-based spit ending in Penrhyn Point, while to the north a wall is based on Ynys Brawd. Upstream the harbour is limited by the railway bridge/viaduct, though there are some moorings above it. Be it noted by owners of wooden hulled boats that the timbers of the bridge are infested by gribble.

As can be seen from the plan, the harbour mostly dries leaving only pools. The Harbour Master locates the main moorings as off Penrhyn Point, and asks that enquires should be made at his office at the quay, which dries but berthing is feasible there. Anchoring is not encouraged because four underwater cables cross the harbour, two of them labelled 'power'. Some recent improvements have been made in protection of the harbour, centred on the little island of Ynys Brawd, and a barrage joins it to the shore, with an extension towards Penrhyn Point, the end of which is lit; this serves to control the run in from the NW. High wind and swell are liable to come in so that the shelter is not so full as the chart would suggest. Exit may be held up by rough water on the bar, and crossing on the ebb should be

*Barmouth.* Harbour frontage against the lowering mountain background. *Author*

*Barmouth.* Most of the moorings are seaward of the railway bridge, as here; there are others above, but access will depend on mast height. *Author*

avoided. There is a good deal of yachting activity but little or no commercial traffic, though previously the port was used for the slate trade. There is a sailing club but no boatyard.

Barmouth is rather gloomily robbed of the morning sun by the hill behind the town, but later in the day comes into its own as a cheerful well-supplied resort. A ferry runs across to Point Penrhyn where there is a miniature railway, while in the hinterland there is good mountain country.

### Aberdovey

There is a port plan in Chart No 1484. After leaving Barmouth and heading for Aberdovey, the Sarn Bych (standing four miles out) has to be remembered. In rough weather it would be advisable to go outside the buoy, though there is otherwise sufficient water to cross direct. A mile north of Aberdovey Outer buoy, offshore small craft moorings are charted, though these are in a very exposed position. The River Dovey runs almost west straight out to sea from an inland lagoon between the usual sandspits. Aberdovey Outer is a mile out from the troublesome bar, which is marked by the Bar Buoy. A considerable stream is generated on the ebb, reaching 3½ knots at springs and reported as running at 6 knots past the jetty in the harbour. The channel buoys are moved as the banks shift, and there are piles and a refuge beacon guarding the spit on the south side.

Anchorage is not permitted in the harbour, no doubt on account of the two marked underwater cables which cross it. Visiting yachts are directed to tie up to the wooden jetty at which there is a least depth of 3m (10 ft) of water. The Harbour Master's office is on the quay behind the jetty, where there are berths which dry at half ebb; there are no public moorings. He will supply barge boards where necessary. There are full supplies, fuel, chandlery and a sailing club all based on a pleasant little town. In settled weather Aberdovey has its advantages for cruising people, but at high water with onshore winds the shelter is not good.

### Aberystwyth

It is unfortunate that the scale of the plan in Chart No 1484 is so small that the layout of the features of the harbour cannot be easily distinguished. Aberystwyth has more protection than many of the Cardigan Bay harbours, though it dries almost throughout; commercial traffic and trawling have however almost gone.

Before approaching from the north another Sarn (Cynfelyn Patches) has to be crossed. There is a main channel charted, but this is not marked and it may be necessary in rough weather to pass outside the Patches buoy; a transit line is charted using the Wellington monument on Pendinas. The leading lights inside the harbour are lit only occasionally. There is the usual troublesome bar, but in settled weather there is three feet (one metre) of water over at half flood with offshore anchorage.

The harbour is formed at the confluence of two rivers. The entrance is protected from the north by a lit embankment, and from the SW by a stone embankment with a more powerful light. It is proposed to extend the northern embankment and Town Quay by a new wooden pile jetty. Visitors are asked to report to the Harbour Master at the Town Quay, who will arrange a berth. Opposite the Town Quay is St David's Quay, which also dries, with the outer end being reserved for visitors. Once in, some swell can be expected round high water with onshore winds. There are private moorings, which dry, higher up the harbour and plenty of small boat and yacht activity with a sailing club on the Town Quay. The harbour is reasonably sheltered and the town is welcoming with much of interest. It is well worth a few days stay, which may be enforced by the behaviour of the bar.

### New Quay (Cardigan)

In the fifteen-miles journey south from Aberystwyth there is no harbour of note. Aberayon might be mentioned as a possibility in fine weather; its shelter is however poor and it holds only a few local fishing boats on significantly heavy moorings. New Quay is an open bay with the main stone wall heading east and a smaller inner wall further to the south giving a little more coverage. There are moorings in the main bay but when the wind veers beyond north west there is a heavy scend. I once spent ten days in New Quay, during which every forecast gave gale warnings for the Irish Sea and the storm cones were never lowered. Mr Winston Evans, the RNLI coxswain, lent me a mooring behind the inner wall on the beach; these are necessarily made up of very heavy fore and aft chains carefully tended. Luckily the gales did not wander much past NW, and only the back-scend from New Quay Bay was troublesome. At the first lull I was able to make my escape by a single handed night passage round to Holyhead, as the nearest place that the boat could be left in relative safety.

### Aberporth

This place is mentioned not because it provides any harbour or shelter, but rather because it is the base for a sea missile establishment. When active, passing boats are escorted along the coast by a guard boat, but it is what is happening out to sea that is much more important. Chart No 1971 carries a deliberately vague warning notice to the effect that targets, moorings and scientific instruments exist within twenty miles of Aberporth. Some are lit and their positions are frequently changed. Older charts showed such buoys but the current issue do not. I do not know whether the range is still operational, but I have had the experience of finding myself near one of the targets when a missile arrived. There were no lateral guard buoys though a recovery vessel was hovering round. At twenty miles off shore a yacht may very well be out of range of radar, and moreover the range cuts across courses between Holyhead or Tremadoc Bay and Fishguard. If therefore uncharted buoys are sighted (and there is plenty of sea room to miss them) in this area, it would be wise to pass well to the west of them. A certain amount of secrecy is natural in missile matters, but this can be of little consolation to the skipper who strays unwarned across a twenty mile sea range.

### Cardigan (St Dogmaels)

This twisting inlet is four to five miles long and dries completely. The channel has no official marks or buoys, and one really does need local information or advice to use it, though there is a fair amount of local yachting activity. In general terms entry is from the NE at Cardigan Island keeping to the eastern side, it narrows at the white hotel (conspic) and, heading south, passes between the E and W sandspits; beyond these the channel moves, but may be perched and there is good shelter. Coming in on four hours flood it should be possible to win up to the drying moorings. By the time he leaves, the thoughtful skipper will have provided himself with a local chart.

### Fishguard

Fishguard is often suggested as one of the significant staging posts for yachts in the Irish Sea, being eighty miles south of Holyhead; this conception is however far from the truth. The visiting yachtsman will be surprised to find that the large harbour supports little yachting activity, for the simple reason that the arc of exposure is too large. The two thousand feet northern breakwater was railway designed and built in 1904. This gives protection round to north, but, as soon as the wind veers, the harbour is fully open from north through east to SE, if not further. This exposes the whole point of the exercise, namely the Irish ferry quay, and hence the need for hauling-off wires. The few mooring buoys need heavy tackle, while yachts will

*Fishguard*. Strumble Head lighthouse seen from the SW. *Author*

probably not carry sufficiently strong gear to hold them in the event of an easterly gale. Thus it is not safe to leave a yacht here and should only be used in settled westerly weather for short stay purposes.

The approaches are clear enough, as the harbour is four miles inside Strumble Head, with the lighthouse easy to pick up except in heavy rain; I have never been fortunate enough to identify the Strumble Head aerobeacon (40 miles range) sited inland of the harbour. The distant landmark is a very unusual three-peaked mountain to the east. There is a strong light on the breakwater head and, if coming down from the north, there is a set out from the land on the ebb. In the harbour there is only a limited anchoring space near the lifeboat slip, but it may be possible to negotiate the use of the RNLI mooring buoy. Here there is a landing slip under the hotel with supplies and chandlery at Goodwick, the main town being further on.

Nevertheless, though Fishguard, like so many other railway harbours, can be

*Fishguard*. The northern breakwater with its light can just be seen at the left of the picture. The Old Harbour, where *Sarahay* is lying to the wall on the right, dries out. *Author*

unkind to yachts, it is certainly strategically placed. In going south one needs to pause here to get the best timing over the tricky and unsheltered next leg to Milford Haven. This turns our attention back to the old harbour in Lower Town, even though this is tidal and may hold up departure. The entrance lies between Saddle Point and Castle Point, where some of the old cannon are still *in situ*. Here the north breakwater gives fair shelter round to the north, while the quay is covered from both west and east. What may give trouble is the back-of-the-harbour wind, or a gale coming down the valley from the south at high water. While I have had a little trouble from this unexpected quarter, my preference is decidedly for the old harbour every time rather than the new. Keel boats can anchor in the entry though not with assured shelter. Lower Town is an unspoiled entity with the sailing club, shops, pubs, and chandlery; the main town is close but up a steep hill. There is no Harbour Master and the occasional rogue trawler may cause trouble.

143

**Fishguard to Milford Haven**

Essential charts are Nos 1973, 1482 and 1478, while No 2878 covers Milford Haven. The course threads its way through or outside sunken headlands, the chart being fearsomely strewn with rocks, rips, strong streams and the absence of any buoys. The four lighthouses of Strumble Head, South Bishop, the Smalls and Skokholm Island give guidance for ships, and the first three have RDF signals. Unless a skipper is prepared to make a passage of sixty miles outside the Smalls, he must wait for smooth weather, a settled forecast, overall daylight, good visibility and the full run of the ebb. This exacting prescription is going to be difficult to fill in full, and a skipper may well have to juggle with the possible passages. High water at Milford Haven is roughly five hours before Liverpool, and at Fishguard four hours ahead, but HW at St Anne's Head and St David's Head are within a few minutes of each other. More detailed information of the streams has to be worked out from the Admiralty Pilot. With exception of Solva, there are no worthwhile harbours en route, only a few small bays with partial shelter.

In general terms the possible routes are:
1. Outside the Smalls.
2. Outside North and South Bishop, and then down to Skokholm Island.
3. Outside Ramsey, Skomer and Skokholm Islands.
4. Through Ramsey and Jack Sounds.

Of these four possibilities I only have personal experience of the last, going through the Sounds, but feel that Course No 3 is probably better; there is more latitude in timing, little extra distance and streams of up to seven knots are avoided. The initial leg is the same for all: sixteen miles to St David's Head, with hardly a vestige of shelter in onshore winds. This is a long approach to the mysteries of the Sounds, and since the ideal time to arrive at the Head is surely HW, the use of the engine is inevitable. This is a remote part of Wales centring on the Cathedral town of St Davids.


*Ramsey Sound*  At the narrowest part, the stream is charted at six knots which means one-way traffic only. Additionally, if there is any strong wind from most directions the Sound is to be avoided by yachts. The entry is wide and the sheltered sector in Porth Melgan under the Head can be noted. Then crossing Whitesand Bay, the sentinals of Gwahan and Gafeiliog can be identified by rough water, and the land comes out again at Point St John. Here the course holds towards the mainland, to leave Ywr Wyn Rock and Horseshoe Rock and their rips to starboard. The yacht is now firmly committed to the two mile narrows of the Sound, and the features are unwinding more rapidly than they can be taken in. The natives are mounted on high power inflatables when lifting their pots.

Looking back on the mainland side, the limited shelter of Porthstinan opens up. Together with the lifeboat there are some motorboat moorings here, running the crossing to Ramsey. Close under Ramsey there is sheltered anchorage from the west, out of the stream. The channel is now showing depths of down to two hundred feet. The course still holds to the mainland side with Shoe Rock to be located ahead.

The Bitches on the Ramsey side are very aptly named, as a great race is thrown up over an underwater reef stretching two cables out from the island; the landing jetty is at its base just to the north. Having left Shoe Rock astern, the yacht is out into the smoother six mile crossing of St Bride's Bay; the large Research Area stretching across the bay is charted with an attached note. This is the first full frontal exposure to the Atlantic swells rolling in by Celtic Sea. There is a feasible and charted anchorage just north of the Bitches and under the island, but the roaring overfalls are likely to disturb sleep.

### Solva

Solva is the only significant sheltered harbour on the exposed coastline of St Bride's Bay though there are some moorings in Porth Clais. Solva is identified by the rocks of Green Scar and Black Scar off-lying, and the houses of the town on the hill behind the harbour, which can be of use if one runs out of time for Jack Sound. The secret of Solva is Black Rock, which lies in the entry like a cork in a bottle, with passage on either hand. It is not always a smooth place, but in settled weather there is a deep pool inside it, scoured by the tides, where there is always water for anchorage. If necessary one can wait here overnight without going into the harbour, which is tidal.

*Solva.* Entrance with Black Rock to port. The moorings are under the village to starboard. *Author*

Black Rk

The inlet is steep-sided with an elbow as a swell-spoiler. As an old small trading port there is a quay, which is reserved for private use. The moorings are all organised by the Boatowners Association with offices on the quay, and they dry to clean sand. A block is reserved for visitors, and it is helpful to write for the Association's guide in advance. There is no need to be tide-bound, for it is possible to drop down to Black Rock before half ebb and anchor until it is time to pass either Sound. Visitors will find Solva a clean and cheerful place with good supplies and services. The main activity seems to be angling parties without any trawler traffic. Visitors are made welcome and there is a sailing club. It is no place for keel boats except in the Black Rock pool.

*Jack Sound*  See plan in Chart No 1482. The fearsome reputation of the Sound depends on a stream reaching seven knots, a safe passage between rocks of no more than a cable, the need for a powerful engine and correct timing, and the bad effect of wind with or over the tide. Having said this, there is no need or compulsion to shoot the Sound, as it perfectly simple to go outside both Skomer and Skokholm Islands, giving them a wide berth because of overfalls. The Admiralty Pilot should be noted as saying that: 'The times at which the streams are stated to begin outside and inside St Bride's Bay, and in Jack and Ramsey Sounds, differ considerably. This information should be used with caution due to incomplete data.' But clearly one can only go with the stream, and a glance astern will show the necessity of keeping steering way.

The approximate course across the Bay from Ramsey Sound is 170°M, the entrance to Jack Sound being difficult to pick out until close in. The signpost is Tuskar Rock which is left to port, there are no beacons. From here the course aims to pass between Cable Rock and the Crabstones, the drying heights of which are charted. If possible, the Crabstones should be given the wider berth as they create the more disturbance. Once through the narrows there is a sense of anticlimax as the smoother water returns.

### Milford Haven

The last five miles of the passage to St Ann's Head are fairly clear. Holding due south from the exit of Jack Sound, the course lies between The Blackstones and The Bench and thence into open water. St Ann's Head is now clear, though high ground obscures the lighthouse. There is no need for a yacht to use the main channel fairway buoys; indeed, there is no need to joust with tankers in the channel at all. The Head is steep-to and the mere yacht can creep diffidently close in. The course passes West Blockhouse, Watwick Point, and finally Dale Point, until entering Dale Flats when the moorings will be in view. There will usually be a vacancy, and ashore there is a slip, boatyard, chandlery, the sailing club and limited supplies. Milford Haven is treated in more detail in the Bristol Channel section.

**Charts**

| No | Title | Scale 1: |
|----|-------|---------:|
| 1121 | Irish Sea with St George's Channel and North Channel. | 500,000 |
| 1410 | St George's Channel. | 200,000 |
| 1478 | St Govan's Head to St David's Head. | 75,000 |
| 1765 | Old Head of Kinsale to Power Head. | 50,000 |
| 1772 | Rosslare and Wexford Harbours with approaches. | 30,000 |
|  | Rosslare harbour. | 10,000 |
| 1773 | Port of Cork: Upper harbour east; upper harbour west. | 12,500 |
| 1777 | Port of Cork: Lower harbour and approaches. | 12,500 |
| 1787 | Carnsore Point to Wicklow Head. | 100,000 |
| 2046 | Waterford Harbour. | 25,000 |
|  | Dunmore East harbour. | 5,000 |
|  | New Ross. | 10,000 |
| 2049 | Old Head of Kinsale to Tuskar Rock. | 150,000 |
| 2053 | Kinsale Harbour and Oyster Haven. | 12,500 |
| 2071 | Youghal Harbour. | 12,500 |
| 2092 | Toe Head to Old Head of Kinsale. | 50,000 |
| 2129 | Long Island Bay to Castlehaven. | 30,000 |
| 2184 | Mizen Head to Gascanane Sound. | 30,000 |
| 2424 | Valentia to Cork. | 152,000 |
| 2740 | Saltee Islands. | 25,000 |

**Milford Haven–Waterford Harbour**

On leaving Milford Haven the choice lies between going north or south of the Smalls lighthouse. Going north, one passes through Broad Sound between Skokholm and Skomer Islands, and a course may be laid direct for the Coningbeg light vessel, with only a very small alteration to pass through the shipping lanes to the west of the Smalls lighthouse. Going south of the Smalls, one can lay a course two miles south of the LH and then alter to cross the shipping lanes at right angles. The route chosen will probably depend on the wind direction if under sail but, whether power or sail, due consideration must be given to the tides, as they run hard between the mainland and the Smalls.

Once clear of the shipping lanes, the next objective is the Coningbeg light vessel. Again the tides must be considered and allowed for. Progress can be checked by the RDF beacons on the South Bishop and the Tuskar Rock lighthouses; it has been my

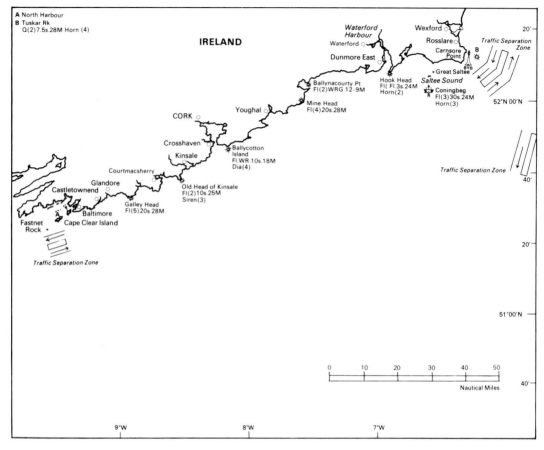

Fig. 27 Rosslare to Cape Clear.

experience that the former has a weak signal and the latter a strong one. On several occasions I have had a worrying grope for the Coningbeg light vessel in poor visibility and have been thankful for a good EP plot. See also Fig 1, page 2.

From the Coningbeg light vessel lay a course to leave Hook Head 1–2 miles to the north; the tides are not so strong here as in the south end of St George's Channel. The water may be seen breaking on the Coningbeg rock. Tower race off Hook Head is caused by the ebb from Waterford meeting the west-going stream off Hook Head, and is worst when the streams are running at their strongest (and can be fierce with a strong SW wind); in fair weather one can pass through it without much bother. Off Hook Head keep a good lookout for lobster pot buoys and salmon nets.

### Rosslare–Dunmore East

If the crossing has been to Rosslare, as described at the beginning of the book, or if the boat is en passage down the east coast of Ireland from the north, the shortest

148

and most interesting route from Rosslare to Dunmore East is via Saltee Sound. For this, clear and settled weather is needed, as navigation is by line of sight with only few buoys en route; Tuskar Rock marine radio beacon lies abeam and can give useful check bearings. The Rosslare buoyed channel is left inshore of the Splaugh Rock buoy, and the coast then followed down to Carnsore Point keeping an eye on the Fundale Rock buoy; Carnsore Point is turned well inside the Barrels buoy. Buoys are now scarce, but there is no lack of unmarked lobster pots so that a lookout on the foredeck is needed. In my view the stranger should avoid the temptation to take the short cut over St Patrick's Bridge, but pass instead through the Saltee Sound. The course to Hook Head is obvious and there is little stream. Basking sharks are commonplace here.

**Waterford Harbour**
Waterford Harbour is a large estuary lying between Hook Head to the east and Dunmore East to the west. You are now in Ireland.

*Dunmore East.* Looking north, showing yachts against the west wharf, with the yacht club above them. *Bob Evans*

*Dunmore East*

Use Chart No 2046, which covers the whole of Waterford Harbour. This is a fishing harbour which is the headquarters for the Waterford pilots. There are often merchant vessels lying off waiting for the tide to go up to Waterford or New Ross; entry should present no problems during night or day. Lay a course for Dunmore Bay leaving the lighthouse on the east pier a cable and a half (275m) to port. The turn-in can be made when the north corner of the west wharf is well open with the end of the east pier extension; do not be tempted to cut the corner, close round the latter, as there are granite blocks lying off it. There are moorings in the SW corner of Dunmore Bay. Berth alongside the NW end of the west wharf, where there are piles and ladders; if you are alongside the piles you will need barge boards. The east pier is mainly for fishing boats and it is inadvisable to lie alongside, as they tend to move in the early hours and return late in the evening. At the SW end of the west wharf, there are the smaller lobster boats, which again move out early in the morning and do not take kindly to yachts lying alongside them.

There are no harbour dues, but one is invited to give a donation to the lifeboat authority whose office is at the south end of the west wharf. Waterford Sailing Club has its clubhouse on the west wharf and they are very welcoming, though they are normally only open on weekday evenings in July and August. There are several hotels and a bus service to Waterford. To change money without going into Waterford, go either to the yacht club or to one of the hotels.

*Cheek Point*

The channel up the river Suir to Cheek Point is well buoyed and quite straight forward. It is used by merchant vessels and, if one is in the channel, be prepared to clear it if a large ship approaches. Do not be tempted to cut the corner off Passage East, as Passage Strand extends to the east of the light on the trellis structure. Once round Buttermilk Point I have found it worthwhile to set in to Shelburne Bay across Carter's Patch, in order to round Cheek Point with the widest berth possible; I have on one occasion come across a merchantman on her way downstream at this point – to the consternation of both vessels. One can anchor off Cheek Point in good holding and there is a good hostelry ashore.

*Cheek Point–Waterford*

The channel up the river Suir to Waterford is well buoyed and easy to follow. The Queen's Channel along the north of Little Island is very narrow, just over half a cable (100m) wide in places, so be prepared to mud hop if a large vessel is in the offing. If in a shallow draft yacht and the tide gives sufficient depth of water, King's Channel is a worthwhile alternative; this is the original course of the river but it has silted up badly at its eastern end, with patches of half a metre at LAT. There is a considerable tidal swirl at the flood where the King's and Queen's channels meet at

150

the western end of Little Island, so care has to be taken of the ship's head. At Ballycar opposite Smelting House Point, there is a heronry which is worth looking out for.

## Waterford

Waterford is a commercial port, the merchantmen for the most part favouring the north side. Berth alongside the floating pontoon downstream of the clocktower. I have found it best to lie facing upstream as there is less stress on the rudder when the ebb is running. There are numerous drinking bars along the waterfront and, being virtually in the centre of town, there is ready access to banks, shops and the like. A yacht normally attracts quite a lot of interest and so, when ashore, take care to make hatches secure. If you have time, one of the tours round the glass works is worth while.

*River Barrow*   The Barrow Bridge has only 6m (20 ft) above MHWS, so the majority of yachts have to have it opened. It is therefore worthwhile telephoning the bridge operator (Waterford 88137) either from Dunmore or Cheek Point, to warn him of your approximate time of approach. The other method is to approach with a flag at the foremast peak and sounding the fog horn. Once the bridge is open, pass through the starboard side, but on the run-up take care to allow for the stream which can be quite strong.

The channel up to New Ross is quite well marked and in general follows the outside of the bends, so do not be tempted to cut corners. Keep a good look-out for shipping and be prepared to leave the buoyed channel. New Ross is a small market town and one can berth alongside the town quay. There is a good selection of shops and I have enjoyed combining a glass of stout with selecting groceries.

## Waterford–Cork

Chart No 2049 covers this passage adequately, Cork being at the western end of the chart; there are larger scale charts if you are putting into Dungarvan (No 2017) or Youghal (No 2071).

## Dunmore–Youghal

The tide is not more than one knot at springs in a NE/SW direction over this 35-mile leg. On leaving Dunmore East, lay a course clear of the Falskirt Rock (dries 3m or 10 ft) off Swines Head and, once abeam, lay a course one mile south of Ram Head. Until Brownstone Head is to the north of you, keep a good look out for salmon fishermen in the season; this area is popular with them. Some 4 miles WSW of Swines Head, Tramore Bay will be open. It is well to study it through the binoculars, as it can be easily misidentified for the entrance to Waterford Harbour when coming from the west in poor visibility. There are three towers on Great

Newton Head on the West side of the bay; on one of these is the Iron Man who points east towards Waterford, to warn vessels in poor visibility that they have got the wrong bay.

The course from Tramore to Mine Head has not got any very easily identified objects to fix on during the day. Ballynacourty Point light is not easily distinguished in daylight, even with a good pair of glasses; but almost immediately behind it is what is called a *Works* on the chart, and this is often giving off a cloud of smoke or dust which can be easily recognised. By night, the course should take one within easy range of the light. With Mine Head to the north, Capel Island should start to come up at the west of Youghal Bay. When Ram Head is to the north, alter towards the east bar.

### Youghal

To enter, shape a course to pass approximately half a mile off Blackball Head, which should put one in the middle of the Youghal lighthouse east bar white sector, one can then alter on to a WNW course for the entrance; minimum depth over the east bar is just over 2m (6 ft 6 ins) at LAT. Once in the middle of the channel, alter

*Youghal*. Looking NNW along the shore. The large building to the left is a convent. *Bob Evans*

152

north; the tidal stream is strong through the entrance: 2.5 kts flood and 3 kts ebb at springs. Though there are several docks (Market and Green Docks); they dry and, at low water, appear rather foul-bottomed and definitely tend to be more than aromatic. One can either lie to an anchor above or just to the east of the end of Ferry Point, or go alongside towards the end of the wall on the western side just above the slip (there are no ladders). Alongside the wall the bottom is sand and pretty clean. However, at the very northern end, it has been reported that a coaster dug quite a hole out of the bottom when trying to get off. The stream, though reported as 2 kts flood and 2.5 kts ebb, appears a lot less alongside. If one opts to lie at anchor off Ferry Point, the service ferry marked on the chart does not run. Therefore, a sound dinghy is necessary.

With a strong southerly wind, the sea breaks on the bars and Youghal should not be attempted. If one is already inside, it can be a bit of a rolling ground in these conditions, and it is better to go above where the old bridge used to be, and lie round the corner on the sand flats at the entrance to the Tourig River, drying 3.1m (10 ft) at LAT.

The town of Youghal is reputed to be the oldest in Ireland and is pronounced Yawl; the name is derived from the Irish Eochaill, meaning Yew Wood. A popular holiday resort with good beaches to the west of Moll Goggins Corner, it was at one time a walled and fortified town and has quite a history, which includes having had Sir Walter Raleigh as its mayor in the 16th century; it is still famous for its broadloom carpet weaving. There is a good selection of hotels, shops and banks.


*Cork*
Depending on draft and the state of tide, one can leave Youghal entrance and lay a course for 3 cables (550m) east of Capel Island across the west bar. Reported depths are just over 1½m (5 ft) at LAT, 7 cables (1300m) south of Moll Goggins Corner. If a greater depth is required, then the east bar should be used. When the Bar Rocks south cardinal buoy is on the port beam, you are clear of danger; do not forget to keep a good look-out for salmon nets. Once round Capel Island lay a course for one mile south of Ballycotton Island (6M); with that abeam, a small alteration of course to starboard brings you to The Smith's buoy (1½M). It is worth going outside this, but once abeam one can either go inside or outside Pollock Rock (6.5M). With the Pollock Rock buoy close abeam, one should be able to see Roche's Point lighthouse on the eastern side of Cork Harbour entrance. Leave this lighthouse 2 cables (350m) to the north, because the Cow and Calf Rocks to the south of the point dry. There is also a wreck off these rocks with a reported depth of just under 4m (13 ft) at LAT. When the entrance is open, one can go up the east channel 1½ cables (275m) wide at outer harbour rock buoy. The channel widens thereafter and, if a large ship has to take precedence, there is sufficient water to the east of E 1 buoy over the Chicago Knoll.

*Capel Island.* Looking west; Knockadown Head is behind the island to its right. *Bob Evans*

## Crosshaven

Chart No 1777 is best, and includes the whole river up to Drake's Pool. From the entrance, cross the channel to within 1½ cables (275m) of Ram's Head and, once round, stay on a WNW heading for buoy C 1, leaving it to starboard, then alter to a SW heading. There are two leading lights set in the garden of the end house off Curraghbinny. The red pile (unlit) should be left to port. Inside this, the water is shallow: 0.5m (1 ft 6 ins) at LAT with a hard gravel bottom. I have tried anchoring inside over the shallows and dragged. Once clear of pile C 2, shape up to the south to leave Curraghbinny pier ½–¾ cable (50–100m) to starboard. Ahead there is a marina where one should be able to find a berth. The river is full of moorings, and three cables (550m) upstream of the marina there is the Royal Cork Yacht Club (on the south bank), which has its own pontoons. I have lain at anchor upstream of these in about 1m (3 ft) over mud; however, there is not much room to swing and it can only be done in shallow draft vessels. If the wind is blowing hard from the west, it can cause quite a little lop in the Owenboy River, in which case it is probably better to go up to Drake's Pool. This is a further 1½ miles up river from the Royal Cork YC, and is where Francis Drake hid from the Spanish in 1587. It is a beautiful, quiet anchorage but quite a step from Crosshaven. The river is tidal, and rowing against the ebb is hard work for more than a short pull.

If one wishes to lie to the Royal Cork YC pontoon, clear it with the Secretary and be prepared to present credentials. The club has a well appointed headquarters, as might be expected from the oldest one in the business (est. 1720), and is rightly jealous of its facilities. It has suffered in the past at the hands of some inconsiderate visitors.

Crosshaven itself has several bars, restaurants and shops. Fuel can be obtained from the garage south of the marina, and the boatyard is able to undertake major repairs.

*East Passage*   If one has time or the weather outside is unfavourable for passage making, a sail over to East Passage is well worthwhile; Chart No 1777 will get you there. Lay a course from Crosshaven making for the gap between Spike Island and the oil terminal off Corkbeg Island. Once clear of the oil terminal jetty, lay a course ENE up the east channel, making first for the head of the bay; the channel is

*East Passage*. Looking north. The church is seen to the right with the marina opposite. *Bob Evans*

155

unbuoyed. Having sailed up the east channel for about half a mile, you should be able to pick out the perch at the Western end of Fair Pock to the north; it can be quite difficult to see at first. When this perch is NNW, alter course further to the north between Marloag and Gold Points. There are cottages on Gold Point, one of which has a white flagstaff and transit for racing. There is plenty of water in East Passage, the shallowest being 6m (20 ft) just off the church on the starboard hand. Opposite this on the port side there is a marina, which has still to be completed, but the pontoons are laid and it is hoped that showers and changing facilities will follow; diesel can be obtained on the pontoons. One cable (180m) upstream on the starboard side is a jetty, where one can lie alongside for short periods to sample the watering hole known as *Dirty Murphy's*. Apart from Murphy's bar there is very little up East Passage, so that this is a most tranquil and attractive creek for those who want peace and quiet away from it all. The nearest shops are in Cobh (pronounced Cove), a good 3½ miles walk away.

### Cork–Baltimore

The passage from Cork to Baltimore – indeed all the way to the south-western tip of Ireland – is covered by Chart No 2424, and there are many larger scale charts of various ports en route.

*Kinsale*. Looking north to the entrance. Charles Fort is just opening from the headland behind Bulman buoy. *Bob Evans*

*Old Head of Kinsale.* Looking west. *Bob Evans*

### Kinsale

On leaving Cork harbour entrance, lay a course S-by-W for Daunt Rock buoy (4M). One can pass inside this, leaving Robert's Head 3 cables (550m) to NW. When Big and Little Sovereign Islands are well open with Reanie's Head, alter to the WSW to pass 2 cables (350m) south of Big Sovereign Island (6.5M). Once Big Sovereign is to the north, alter onto W-by-S to leave the Bulman Rock buoy to starboard. Once clear of the Bulman Rock buoy alter onto N-by-W until Charle's Fort has opened. Charle's Fort has a sectored light and at night the white sector should be used initially until comfortably inside the Heads, and then the white or green sectors. Two cables (350m) south of Charle's Fort there is a bar with a least depth of 3.1m (10ft) at LAT.

Leave Charle's Fort 1½ cables (275m) to starboard and keep to the outside of the bend, leaving the Spur and Spit buoys to port. The town of Kinsale will be open to the west of Blockhouse Point. There is a marina at the town pier, or one can anchor off the southern end of the town either on the town side or to the east off Castle Park. The Kinsale Yacht Club overlooks the town pier and is very hospitable; showers are available. Kinsale itself is a sizeable town, with a good chandlery and fuel can be obtained from the shark fishing centre by Customs quay; there also is a launderette just along from the yacht club. If staying for several days, Oyster Haven and Sandy Cove are worth a visit.

### Kinsale–Glandore

Chart No 2092 is more detailed than No 2424. The passage from Kinsale to Old Head of Kinsale is quite straightforward. Off the east of Old Head there is Bream Rock (steep to); the race extends SW on the ebb and SE on the flood from Old Head.

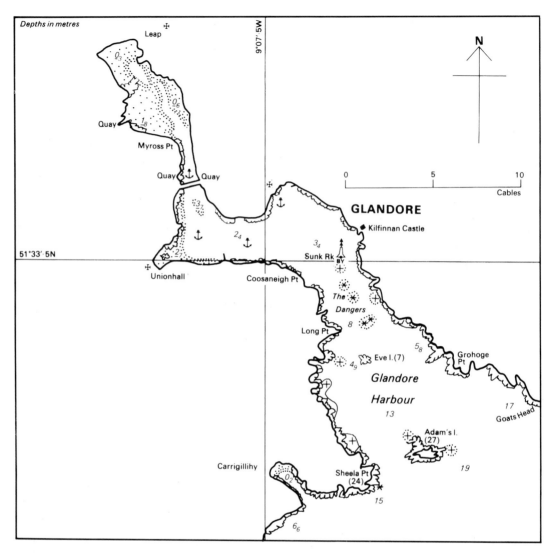

Fig. 28 Glandore Harbour.

The maximum spring rate can reach 2½ kts, so it is fairly important to work the tides. There is an inside passage avoiding the race but, with the tide running hard and a strong wind, it is advisable to give the Head at least 2 miles berth. From Old Head of Kinsale lay a course WSW for the Seven Heads (the name refers to seven castles not seven heads); keep a good watch for salmon nets, as this appears to be a popular area in June and July. Off Seven Heads, the tidal stream can run as much as 2 kts at springs. From here lay a course across Clonakilty Bay for a mile south of Galley Head. Half a mile SW of Galley Head Light there is an unmarked rock

Dhulic, which is awash at HW. 1½ cables (275m) south of Dhulic is the Sink Rock, which again should be given a wide berth. Once clear of these two dangers, an alteration on to W-by-N brings you up to Glandore.

## Glandore

Enter between Sheela Point and Goats Head; Adam Island lies plum in the entrance. Approaching from the east, leave Adam Island to port, keeping midway between it and Goats Head. Just over a quarter of a mile (500m) past Adam Island lies Eve Island, which can be left either to port or starboard. If port, take a course closer to Eve Island than the eastern shore. Just over a cable (200m) past Eve, there is the Outer Danger marked by perches to the east and west. Leave the Danger to starboard, passing between it and Long Point. A further cable (180m) on, there is the Middle Danger which should be left to starboard; ¾ cable (140m) on again is the Inner Danger, marked by a perch. To the north of the Inner Danger lies Sunk Rock marked by a north cardinal buoy. None of Adam, Eve, Outer, Middle,

*Glandore.* Eve Island is to the right; Outer, Middle and Inner Dangers run to the left, with Sunk Rock beyond. The village is left of picture. *Bob Evans*

Inner Dangers or Sunk Rock is lit. At the head of the bay lies Glandore, a drying harbour with a stone jetty. Anchorage is good in sand, but with winds from the south or south east, it is somewhat exposed, though some protection is afforded by Adam, Eve and the Dangers. However, better shelter can be obtained off Union Hall, which is half a mile to the west.

Glandore is a small village mostly engaged in the holiday trade. It has one hotel on the waterfront, from which one can obtain petrol, and one other bar. There is a small chandlery.

### Castletownsend

From Glandore, Castletownsend or Castle Haven is only 4½ miles. Having cleared Adam Island, make a course SSW for High Island, passing inside or outside it. If going inside, make sure of clearing to the south of Belly Rock, 1½ cables (275m) south of Rabbit Island (which has a host of small rocks off its eastern end, so keep clear of it in any event). Once clear of High Island, Low Island, Seal Rocks and Row Rock, lay a course for Horse Island south of the entrance to Castle Haven. When two cables (350m) south of Skiddy Island, alter for Battery Point, and when Reen Point is abeam alter to the NW, between Battery and Reen points. Reen has a light on it which is sectored, so that red guards Horse Island and Black Rock, and green guards Skiddy Island.

Take the mid-channel up the river, keeping clear of Reen Point's western side, and of Colonel Rock. Just over half a mile up river one can anchor in 3m (10 ft) at LAT off the village of Castletownsend, which lies on the western shore with a good mud holding ground. If the wind is in the south, this can be rather exposed, and more shelter can be found further up river towards Raheen Castle, where there is a shingle bank extending from the eastern shore. Inside this it dries, so that only those boats which can take the ground can hide behind it.

Castletownsend takes its name from the Townsend family who still live in the castle, once the home of Edith Somerville of the famous Somerville and Ross partnership who wrote *The Stories of an Irish RM*; the village's real delight is its tranquility. There are several shops in the village, and two bars; *Mary Ann's* is renowned for its seafood cooking. The church is worth visiting as it is full of Anglo-Irish history.

### Castletownsend–Baltimore

When clear of Battery and Reen points, lay a SSE course between Skiddy Island and Black Rock off Horse Island. Once Black Rock bears west, alter for Skullane Point, giving it a reasonable offing to clear the small island and a ledge from the mainland which extends half a cable (100m). Having cleared Skullane Point, one can either go inside or outside the Stags. These are spectacular rocks 66 ft (20m) high which lie ¾-mile off Toe Head; from either east or west these look very like a vessel under sail. The channel between Toe Head and the Stags is deep and free of danger,

160

*Baltimore Harbour.* Looking West, with Sherkin Island in the background, nearing low water. *Bob Evans*

but there can be quite a sea in fresh westerly winds. The stream is appreciable both inside and outside the Stags, so it is advisable to have it favourable. Once clear of Toe Head and the Stags, lay a course to pass south of Kedge Island for, though there is a deep channel between Carrigthru Rock and mainland, it is safer to go outside, especially if there is any sea running.

Leave Kedge Island ½-mile to the north, as there is a race extending from its SW tip; the stream can be up to 2 kts. Once Kedge is clear to the NE, and the white beacon on the eastern side of Baltimore Harbour entrance has opened with Black Point, alter on to WNW for a position 2 cables (350m) south of Beacon Point. There is a light on Barrack Point, and the white sector extends up to Black Point so, if one turned immediately in the white sector when coming from the east, one would come to disaster on Whale Rock. The white beacon on the eastern side of the entrance is unlit but conspicuous in daylight; it is known as Lot's Wife.

### Baltimore Harbour

The southern entrance is just over a cable (200m) wide, the harbour being almost landlocked and protected on its western side by Sherkin Island. In the southern entrance, Loo Rock is marked by a buoy, half a cable (90m) off Beacon Point, and

161

one should enter keeping the buoy close to starboard. Having passed Loo buoy, do not be tempted to come to starboard close to Connor Point on Coney Island, as there is Quarry Rock with just 2m (6 ft 6 ins) over it at LAT. Head up towards the perch (south cardinal marks) in the middle of the bay until Coney Island lies to the east, and Baltimore Harbour is open with the north tip of Coney Island. There are yacht moorings from the harbour to Coney Island. Anchorage off Baltimore outside the yacht moorings is good holding ground.

If there is a blow from the north, a quieter anchorage can be found to the north of Baltimore village under Ringarory Island; similarly from the west under Sherkin Island off Abbey Strand. It is possible to get alongside the north wall outside the harbour, and some small yachts go inside the south wall. The north wall is used by trawlers, and there can also be disturbance early in the morning on the south wall from the Clear Island and Sherkin ferries. On no account moor alongside the west wall as it has foul ground. If able to dry out, the bay formed by Coney Island has a firm and fair bottom at its head and mud further out. A decent four point moor can easily be established, giving a clean walk ashore.

Baltimore village has one hotel, *Baltimore House*, where a good meal can be had and also a bath in the afternoon; there are also several bars and restaurants. The place survives on yachting, tourism, boat building and fishing, and during August is very busy. Diesel can only be obtained from the fishermen at the harbour, and petrol from a garage about a mile out on the Skibbereen road. Repairs can be undertaken at the yard 1½ cables (275m) NW of the harbour. There are several shops for provisions, one of which has some chandlery. There are no permanent banks, but both Allied Irish and the Bank of Ireland have a caravan once a week. Any major shopping has to be done at Skibbereen, an attractive trip by road but some 8 miles.

### Roaringwater Cruise

In settled weather one could cruise for weeks in Long Island and Roaringwater bays, with the backdrop of Mount Gabriel to the north. Assuming that time is limited, I shall describe a basic cruise of the area.

### *Baltimore–Cape Clear Island*

Leave Baltimore by the south entrance and, once clear of Wilson Rocks off Sherkin, lay a course SW for Gascanane Sound – this lies between Sherkin and Cape Clear Island. There are several dangers, namely Badger Island and Crab Rocks off Sherkin, and also Carrigmore Rocks. 'Best Channel' is, however, just under 3 cables (500m) wide and is better than the passage between Gascanane Rock and Cape Clear Island which is only just over a cable (200m) wide. Gascanane Rock dries 2m at LAT. Both channels have plenty of water in them, but the streams run up to 3 kts at springs and cause strong eddies close to the rocks. In strong SE winds there is a nasty sea in the sound when the flood is running. It is best to choose a time for going through when the tide serves and the wind is not too fresh.

162

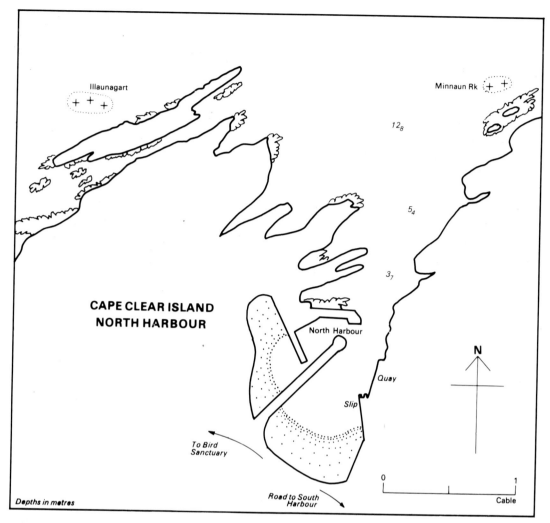

Fig. 29 Cape Clear Is, North Harbour.

Once through the Sound, alter on to a WNW heading to clear Bird Island by 3 cables (550m) to the north. 1½ cables (275m) north of Bird Island there are rocks which are awash at LW, with the Bullig Reef extending nearly 2 cables (350m) W-by-N from them. Once clear of Bird Island and Bullig Reef, alter to SW for Illaunagart at the entrance to North Harbour. Doonamore Castle should be visible further along the coast.

*North Harbour* This is a very small harbour, the approach being made between Illaunagart to the west and Minnaun Rock to the east. The entrance between the jetty and the eastern side is barely 50m wide, and there is an inner and an outer

163

*Clear Island.* Looking SSW into North Harbour at low water. *Bob Evans*

harbour. The inner harbour dries and in bad weather is closed off by baulks of timber; the outer is shallow towards the head. Both appear to have a fair bottom. Yachts not wishing to dry out should secure at the outer end of the jetty, whereas those able to take the ground can go further up the jetty to the last steps; the mid-portion of the jetty is reserved for the mailboat. In rough weather there is a considerable scend in the harbour.

Cape Clear Island has some very beautiful walks, one of the best being to the old lighthouse on the south side. The island is a centre for learning the Irish language, and a large number of young people visit it each year. Close by North Harbour there is a flourishing pottery and enamelling shop. There are three bars, the one close to the harbour having folk singing until all hours. There is one shop a little up from North Harbour which has limited provisions. The roads are rough and narrow, and several Volkswagen Beetles use them; at night they only use one headlamp and appear like angry bouncing cyclops, so the visitor should be prepared. The renowned Fastnet Rock with its powerful lighthouse lies some five miles to the south west.

164

*Cape Clear Island–Crookhaven*
On leaving North Harbour, the passage across Long Island Bay is straightforward with no dangers; look out for lobster pots. The tidal streams set east and west at 1½ kts at springs.

*Crookhaven Harbour*   The entrance to Crookhaven lies between Alderman Island and Sheenan Point and is three cables (550m) wide. The lighthouse on Rock Island is conspicuous with its associated white buildings. Coming from the SE, a course should be laid to leave Alderman Island just under 2 cables (350m) to the south in order to clear Black Horse Rocks (marked with a perch), which lie one cable (180m) north of the island. At night the red sector of the lighthouse guards the Alderman Rocks. Once clear of the Black Horse Rocks, alter on to a W-by-S course up to Crookhaven. Anchorage can be found in just 2m (6 ft 6 ins) at LAT off the village on the port side in good holding ground. If the wind goes into the east, shelter can be found just north of the western end of Rock Island.

Crookhaven is idyllic when it is fine, but it can be rather grey and sombre in dull

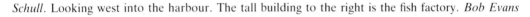

*Schull.* Looking west into the harbour. The tall building to the right is the fish factory. *Bob Evans*

or bad weather. The village is small with one hotel on the waterfront; this has been rebuilt since being destroyed by fire, and offers shower facilities for yachtsmen. There are several bars, of which *Sullivan's* is the best known, and one general store; there is a good stretch of beach. There is not much depth of water at the head of the harbour (one metre at LAT), but the bottom is fair and very gently shelving. Having taken a multihull up there, almost to the water's edge, I was once asked which road I was looking for. On the north shore, opposite the village, are long-abandoned mine workings with, at the entrance, some ex-Admiralty buildings which are relics of the old Royal Navy base of yesteryear.

### Crookhaven–Schull

On leaving Crookhaven lay a course for Barrel Sound. At the western entrance to the Sound lies Duharrig Island, which should be left to starboard. On the northern side is Castle Point and Green Island. In poor visibility the castle ruins on the point are the only positive identification of the correct gap. Lay a course mid-channel, 2 cables (350m) wide, leaving Dromadda and Goat Island to starboard. As Goat Island comes abeam, Long Island Sound will open. The stream runs at 1½ kts in the Sound at springs, but the water is sheltered. Just one mile east of Coney Island, Cush Spit extends 2 cables (350m) from Long Island, and is marked by a buoy. With Cush Spit buoy abeam, Schull Harbour starts to open to port. During the month of August there is excellent mackerel trolling up the sound.

### Schull Harbour

This is the bay to the north of the east end of Long Island Sound, and is well sheltered in all weather except southerly gales. East of Schull Point is Bull Rock, which is covered at half tide and marked by a perch. At night entrance can easily be made by using the leading lights and Copper Point light on Long Island; the leading marks by day are very difficult to see. The entrance is 2 cables (350m) wide between the Bull and Cosheen Point. Off Cosheen Point there are rocks extending nearly a cable (180m), so give it a wide berth.

Anchorage can be made at the head of the bay on the west side, but be sure to be clear of the permanent moorings and leave a clear passage for the fishing vessels. Yachts do lie to the outside of the harbour wall, but only temporarily while taking on water or stores; it is also used by the Cape Clear Island boat and is not advised for visitors.

The town is a small market town and has plenty of shops and two hotels; there is a fish packing station in the harbour, and buses run daily to Skibbereen and Cork. The Harbour Master is most helpful, and fuel can be obtained from one of the garages close to the harbour.

### Schull–Baltimore

On leaving Schull between the Bull and Cosheen Point, lay a course for 1½ cables (275m) east of Copper Point lighthouse on Long Island; once Copper Point is abeam, pick up the Amelia Rock buoy and leave it to port. To save sailing round

166

*Long Island.* Looking SW at Copper Point light. To the right is Long Island Sound – the Irish not the American version. *Bob Evans*

Calf Island, one can pass between the Middle and East Calf: pick up and identify Carthy Island, East, Middle and West Calf Islands, and then head S-by-E until Badger Island off Sherkin is open with the west end of East Calf Island; this will keep you clear of Carthy Island. Enter the passage midway between East and Middle Calf Islands on a southerly heading; it has a good depth of water, except that there is a rocky tail extending 1½ cables (275m) SW from the SW tip of East Calf, so give it a wide berth. Once clear of the East Calf, lay a course SE for Badger Island, and then south between Badger and Carrigmore Rocks. The streams runs at 3 kts during springs, so it is best to have them in your favour as you work your way back to Baltimore.

## XIII Welsh Side of the Bristol Channel (and Severn Estuary)

**Charts**

| *No* | *Title* | *Scale* 1: |
|---|---|---|
| 1076 | Linney Head to Oxwich Point. | 75,000 |
| 1161 | Swansea Bay. | 25,000 |
| 1165 | Worms Head to Watchet. | 75,000 |
| 1167 | Burry inlet. | 25,000 |
| 1176 | Severn Estuary – Steep Holm to Avonmouth. | 40,000 |
| | Newport. | 20,000 |
| | Redcliffe Bay. | 25,000 |
| 1179 | Bristol Channel. | 150,000 |
| 1182 | Barry and Cardiff roads with approaches. | 25,000 |
| | Barry docks. | 12,500 |
| | Cardiff docks. | 15,000 |
| 1478 | St Govan's Head to St David's Head. | 75,000 |
| 1482 | Plans on the coast of south west Wales: | — |
| | Tenby and Saundersfoot with approaches. | 25,000 |
| | Ramsey Sound, with the Bishops and Clerks. | 25,000 |
| | Jack Sound. | 12,000 |
| 2878 | Approaches to Milford Haven. | 25,000 |
| 3274 | Milford Haven – St Ann's Head to Newton Noyes pier. | 12,500 |
| Book | *Bristol Channel Yachting Conference Handbook* (See bibliography) | |

**Milford Haven**

Milford Haven is a busy commercial complex, with large tankers coming and going regularly. The entrance, however, is wide enough to accommodate these and the casual visiting yacht at the same time, for the pleasure seeker can creep close inshore, east or west, depending which anchorage is the destination.

The entrance lies between St Ann's Head to the west and Sheep Island to the east. At its narrowest it is one mile wide, and it is divided into two deep water channels, east and west, the main one being the west. In the centre of the entrance are the Middle Channel and Chapel Rocks with least depths of 5.2m (17 ft) and 3.5m (11 ft 6 ins) respectively. With a fresh SW wind and an ebb tide out of Milford meeting a crossing stream at the entrance, the water can be quite rough. The West Channel has two sets of leading lights, the first being on West Blockhouse and

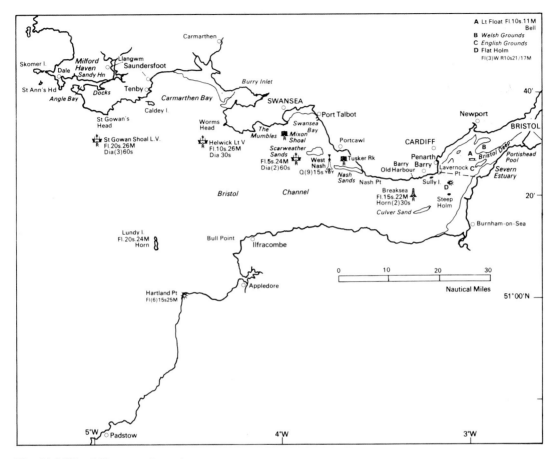

Fig. 30 Milford Haven to Bristol.

Watwick Points, and the second being on Great Castle and Little Castle Heads. St Ann's lighthouse is sectored white, red and intense red; the red sector guards the Gowan Shoal to the south east, and the intense red guards Linney Head and its off-lying unlit rocks. Entry is straightforward, given the correct chart, but an ear should be kept open for Milford Signals on VHF Channel 12 to establish any traffic.

## Dale

Dale is one of the most favoured small boat anchorages, and is well protected from the south and west, but not from the east. The bottom is sand and a good holding ground, but shallow with extensive drying flats towards the beach. If a vessel is able to take the ground happily, she can go almost up to the shingle beach and dry out. Otherwise, to remain afloat one must anchor well out.

There is a yacht yard and a chandlery, as well as a pub, a small store and a sailing club, which is welcoming (and has showers).

169

## Sandy Haven

Sandy Haven is a delightfully secluded creek on the north side of the Haven, just in from Dale. It can be entered 1½ hours before HW by vessels of 1m (3 ft 3 ins) draft but, like many of the harbours along this coast, it is only suitable for boats which can take the ground comfortably. The detail on Chart No 3274 is insufficient to make an entry without first lying off to survey the ground on foot and ascertain the channel. To remain clear of Bull Rock, keep the houses with shingle top stories with Sleeping Bay Point, and the moored boats close to port, following the bed of the creek as surveyed on foot.

The village of Herbrandston is ¾ mile to the east and can be reached by either of the roads. It has a small store, a hotel and a pub/restaurant; this last has a good name for Italian cooking.

## Angle Bay

Angle Bay is situated to the south of the Esso refining jetty. A good anchorage is obtained off Angle Point, with a landing by the old lifeboat house and slip. There are two pubs and a hotel, plus a small store and garage.

## Milford Docks.

Milford Docks can be entered at 2 hours before HW, but they are expensive and dirty to lie in. It is both cheaper and preferable to lie outside to the east of the dock gates on Milford Shelf, with a landing place at the slip to the east of the dock. The town has good shops and a railway station.

## Hobb's Point

Just above Pembroke Dock there is Hobb's Point, where there are yacht moorings off the south bank of the Haven. A mooring may be obtained there by applying to Kelpie Boat Services at the slip. Kelpie's are able to undertake repairs and maintenance.

## Lawrenny Yacht Station

This is just at the entrance of the Carew River, and there are a number of moorings laid off it. There is a small yard with fuel and a neighbouring hotel. The stream tends to run quite hard through the moorings.

## Llangwm

A small village just south of where the river divides into east and west Cleddau. Anchorage is just off the entrance of Llangwm Pill in mud, with a landing at Black Tar Point. The village is a small one, having a post office, a general store and one pub.

### Milford Haven Eastwards

The passage between Milford Haven and Carmarthen or Swansea is notable for the tide race off St Govan's Head, and overfalls at St Gowan Shoals which lie 2 nm to the south. There is a least depth over the latter of 6 metres (20 ft), but the sea breaks over the shoals and there can be tide rips extending up to five miles eastwards, with short seas when wind is against tide. St Gowan Shoals are not marked by buoys directly, but there is a light vessel (Fl 20s 12m 26M) with diaphone (3) two miles to the south; the spring tidal stream off St Govan's Head runs NE/SW at up to 3 knots. Because there is practice firing most weekdays in the summer out to sea between Linney Head and St Govan's Head, it is best to stay 5 miles off shore, and thus St Gown LV makes a good waypoint to clear the range and the shoals (firing can occasionally extend to 10 nm; telephone Castlemartin 262 or Manorbier 281 for details).

### Tenby

Caldey Island lies 2½ nm south of Tenby and has a lighthouse (Fl (3) WR 20s 65m 14M) with a white tower, on its SE tip; there is a conspicuous monastry with a white tower in the middle of the island. The bottom shoals to the east of the island, and there are various drying rocks to the east and north, in particular Woolhouse Rocks one mile NE (drying 2.7m (9 ft) and marked by an unlit south cardinal buoy), and a further rock which lies awash at chart datum one mile due east of Caldey Light. The passage through Caldey Sound is possible by day for shallow draught vessels, which

Fig. 31 Tenby.

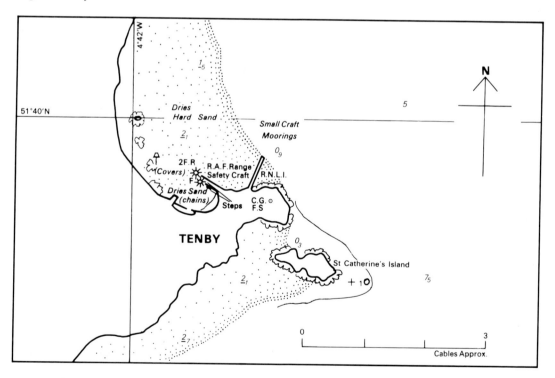

*Tenby*. Looking south at low water. Gosker Rock in the foreground never covers, but the small rock marked by a beacon to the right of the picture covers. *Water-Wise*

*Saundersfoot*. Looking NNE at low water. *Water-Wise*

should stand off from drying sands and rocks south of Tenby; the tidal stream in the sound runs at up to 2½ knots ENE/WSW on the flood and ebb respectively; open anchorage in Caldey Roads gives shelter from all but the north-east, though it is never particularly calm.

Give a wide berth to St Catherine's Island which lies 100m SE of Castle Hill, for there are outlying rocks for a further 100m out to sea. The harbour itself dries out to hard sand (some ladders at the walls) but north-east of the harbour there is good holding ground (which dries out for 400m or ¼-mile); the harbour may be entered by shallow draught vessels at half tide. The tidal range is up to 7½m (25 ft) springs and 3½m (11 ft 6 ins) neaps. A full range of shops and pubs is handy.

**Saundersfoot**
See Tenby above for approach. After passing Tenby, give a good offing to Monkstone Point with its off-lying rock. Enter harbour between the two breakwaters (Fl R to port) in a southerly direction (see photo for channel – but this tends to

Fig. 32 Saundersfoot.

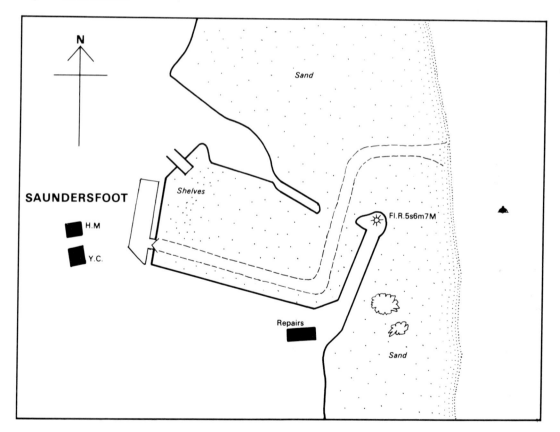

shift), above half tide. There are plenty of ladders at the wall, and the harbour dries out to firm sand. The port is crowded in summer, but the shops are extremely handy to the attractive harbour.

**Carmarthen Bay**

There are various other small harbours and anchorages in Carmarthen Bay; they nearly all dry out, and the waters are subject to strong tidal streams and shifting sands. In particular Carmarthen Bar can be extremely difficult; the admirable *Bristol Channel Yachting Conference Handbook* advises taking local advice before crossing it.

**Swansea Bay**

The passage for small craft to or from Swansea Bay westward lies within ½ nm of Helwick LV (Fl 10s 12m 26M), which guards the SW end of Helwick Shallows; these have a least depth of one metre and are marked at their western end by a west cardinal buoy. The track between Milford Haven and Swansea Bay lies east/west just south of the shallows, between Helwick LV and St Gowan LV to clear the firing range already described. The western approach to Swansea Bay lies between Helwick LV and West Helwick (west cardinal) to leave the shallows to the north, and passes ½ nm south of Helwick Pass (east cardinal) off Porteynon Bay. Anchorage in the middle of the latter offers protection from the north and west in good holding ground off a rocky shore flanking a sandy beach; if going eastward on the ebb, it may be better to shelter here rather than proceed round Oxwich Point into the better protection of Oxwich Bay until the tide serves, because there are overfalls off the point. The mariner should note that the wreck of the *Prince Ivanhoe*, marked at the western end of Porteynon Bay broke up into several large sections during 1981, and forms a danger to small craft using the bay. It lies at 50°32'.7N, 04°11'.8E, approximately ½ mile NNE of the position marked on Chart No 1165 (1979 edition).

Swansea Bay can be said to be bounded by Mumbles Head (Fl (4) 10s 35m 17M Dia (3) 60s) with its rocks and the Mixon Shoal or Bank (dries nearly a metre or 3 feet) to the west, and Scarweather Sands (dries up to 3 metres (10 ft) for a distance of 2 miles) to the south. If going into or out of the bay from or to the westward, in all but fine weather above half tide, pass south of Mixon Bell buoy (red lateral) one mile south of the headland to clear the shoal, and give Mumbles Head, and the off-lying Cherrystones 300m (330 yds) east of it, a wide berth by keeping the Inner Green Grounds south cardinal buoy close aboard. Passage between Mixon Shoal and Mumbles Head may be negotiated by shallow draft vessels in fine weather above half tide, by keeping between 300–400m (330–440 yds) off the Coastguard Station and the same off the lighthouse to pass inside the shoal.

If entering or leaving Swansea Bay to or from the east below half tide, pass to the west of Scarweather Sands (west cardinal) and beware of being set onto the Sands if the tide is flooding. Passage by Kenfig Patches is possible for craft drawing up to two

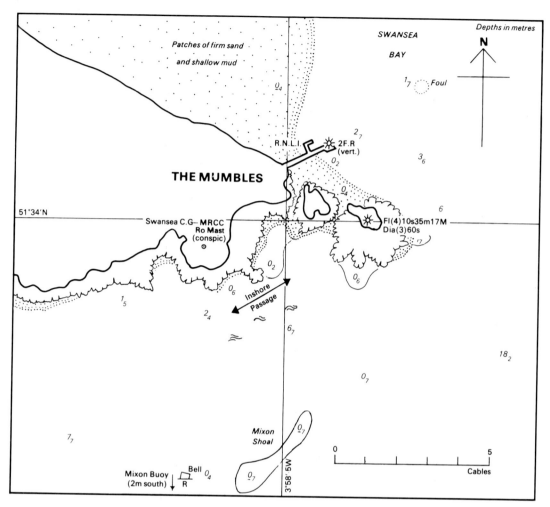

Fig. 33 The Mumbles. With Mixon Shoal.

metres at half tide, but pass to the east of the east cardinal buoy at the Patches themselves, thence to Porthcawl (overfalls at the point), or via Nash Passage if going further eastwards on the making tide (see below under *Barry*). The tidal stream runs up to 5 knots at springs all along this coast.

**The Mumbles**

Firm mud which dries. Yacht club and public slips are approachable three hours either side of high water. The pier (2 FR vert) has 2m (6 ft 6 ins) depths at MLWS, but may not be used by pleasure craft. See under *Swansea Bay* above for passage between Mixon Shoal and Mumbles Head.

*Mumbles Head*. Mixon Shoal half an hour before LWS, looking south from the shore. The inshore passage can be seen where the fisherman is passing, and Mixon buoy is in the left background. *Water-Wise*

### Swansea

 Swansea is a commercial harbour with little room for pleasure craft; permission to enter must be obtained from the Harbour Master (Swansea Dock Radio on Ch 14). The entrance channel is dredged to 3m (10 ft), and craft drawing up to 1¾ metres (5 ft 9 ins) can usually reach the lock to King's Dock at all states of the tide.

 From the SW Inner Green Grounds (south cardinal) buoy one mile east of Mumbles Head, make 020°T for the Outer (QG) and then the Inner (Fl G 2.5s) Fairway buoys (both starboard lateral), and then to the Eastern Breakwater (2 FG vert) before bearing to port up the River Tawe, which dries out to mud. Half a mile beyond King's Dock lies the South Dock with berths for pleasure craft (marina under construction 1982). The yacht clubhouse is close to the South Dock entrance on the north side, but shops are a little way away.

### Port Talbot

Entry to the iron ore terminal with its impressive moles is prohibited to small craft, but the outer channel is well buoyed (laterals) and has leading lights on 060°T (Oc R

176

*Swansea.* Looking south at low water. *Water-Wise*

*Port Talbot.* Looking WSW over the mouth of the river Afon at low water. *Water-Wise*

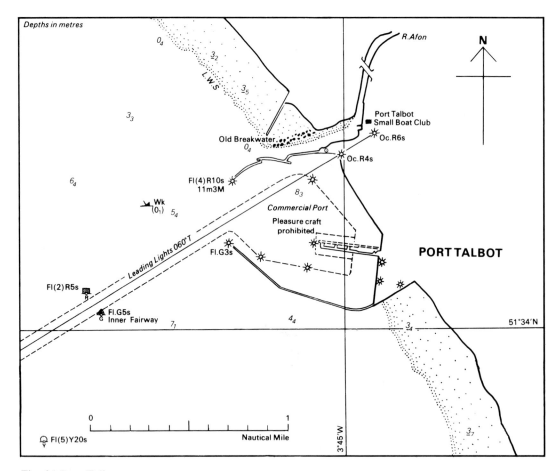

Fig. 34 Port Talbot.

6s and Oc R 4s) which will enable the navigator to approach the entrance to the River Afon just to the north of the terminal, leaving the northern arm of the terminal (Fl (4) R 10s) to starboard. There is a wreck ½ mile due west of the terminal entrance, which is nearly awash at MLWS. There is not much water in the River Afon at LW springs, and often breakers on the bar; entry is best left until 2 hours after LW. The tidal range is up to 8½ metres (28 ft) springs and 4 metres (13 ft) neaps. The yacht club is situated to starboard just after entry to the river, but shops are a short walk away.

**Porthcawl**

If on passage to or from Porthcawl, Scarweather Sands are marked by cardinal and lateral buoys and, with Hugo Bank to the north, should be given a wide berth. Worms Head open of Porteynon Point (292°T) leaves Scarweather Sands to the

178

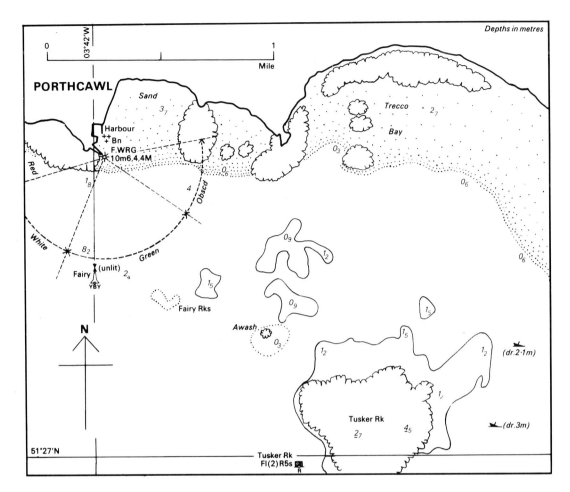

Fig. 35 Porthcawl.

north, passing between West Scarweather (west cardinal) to the north, and Scarweather Lightship (Fl 5s 12m 24M) to the south. Porthcawl entry or departure lies between 035/080°T (approach) or 215/260°T (departure); the WRG light on the breakwater shows white in this sector, and the tidal stream sets at right angles. Passage between Scarweather Sands and Hugo Bank is inadvisable for small craft in all but the best of weather. The channel is buoyed by lateral marks (buoyage direction east), and the line is denoted by a transit of the very tall St Hilary Radio mast (346m (1140 ft) marked by fixed red lights, with one powerful flashing red light at the top) 10 miles east of Porthcawl, in line with Porthcawl Light in its red sector on 095°T; vessels should pass close to North Scarweather buoy (stbd lateral) and then ½ mile north of East Scarweather (east cardinal) on this line and then head south for Porthcawl Light's white sector, giving the overfalls off the Hutchwns Point

*Porthcawl.* Looking SSE at low water. Note the collapsed east wall and marker post just outside the entrance. *Water-Wise*

*Porthcawl.* The same scene at half-tide. *Ogwr Borough Council*

180

a wide berth and remembering that the tide sets fiercely along the coast (up to 6 knots off Porthcawl harbour). If approaching from the east, see below under *Barry (Nash Passage)*. Final approach to Porthcawl harbour may be made in the white sector, between 035°T and 080°T, Tusker Rock lies just over a mile SE of the harbour and dries; Fairy Buoy (unlit west cardinal) guards the western limit of the outlying rocks from Tusker, including Fairy Rock (awash).

Porthcawl harbour dries to soft mud three hours either side of high water and lies inside a western breakwater (lighthouse F WRG 9m; white tower on black base), and a partly collapsed east wall. There are over 30 permanent moorings with attendant ground chains, and 3 visitors berths; visitors may tie up alongside the east wall (some ladders) and should report to the Harbour Master. The collapsed southern portion of the east wall is marked by a post, which must be left to starboard on entry once inside the western breakwater. The tidal range is up to 9 metres (30 ft) springs and 4 metres (13 ft) neaps. A full range of shops and restaurant is handy.

Fig. 36 Barry. With old harbour.

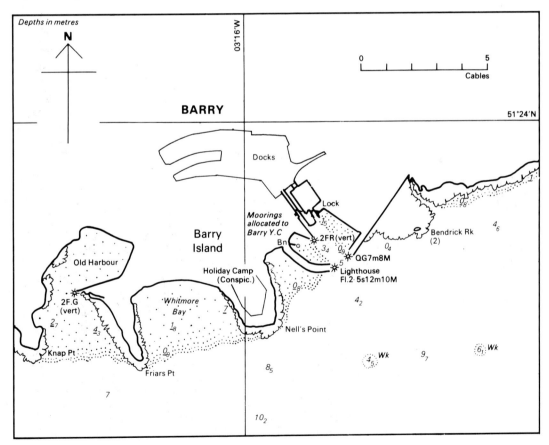

**Barry**

If working Barry to or from the west, small craft should wait until the tide serves as there is a 5 knot stream at springs. Nash Sands extend 8 nm from the Point of the same name, and are marked at their western extremity by West Nash (west cardinal VQ (9) 10s) and overfalls, and at Nash Point by East Nash (east cardinal VQ (3) 5s).

*Nash Passage.* Passage to or from Porthcawl inside Nash Sands is possible in fair weather for small craft, but the channel is only 200 metres (220 yds) wide at its narrowest point. Going south from Porthcawl, leave Tusker lateral port buoy (Fl (2) R 5s) to port and line up Nash Point with the disused lighthouse behind it on 126°T until East Nash (east cardinal) bears 160°T half a mile; pass within 50 metres of East Nash off Nash Point, and steer SE until clear of the headland and overfalls. Reverse the procedure if making for Porthcawl, and always beware of strong tidal streams and overfalls, especially at springs.

*Barry.* Looking SE through the entrance. The commercial docks are left of picture, and yacht moorings are in the foreground. *Water-Wise*

The coastline between Nash Point and Barry is clear of obstacles half a mile to seaward, but note that a concrete tower (Fl R) stands half a mile off Breaksea Point. From the east, keep at least ½ mile offshore to clear rocks and Sully Island. Give all headlands a wide berth along this coast due to rocky outcrops and strong overfalls.

Barry Harbour lies between two breakwaters on the east of Barry Island; there is a westerly set across the entrance at all states of the tide. The western pier has a light (Fl 2.5s 10M) on a white column; the eastern light is QG 8M. This is a commercial harbour and there is water in the main channel at all states of the tide (the rest dries to thick mud at low water), but prior warning is advisable if staying overnight as there are no visitors' moorings; there is a marina inside No 1 Dock. The small bays to east and west dry out, and the tidal range is up to 11½m (38 ft) springs and 6m (20 ft) neaps. Barry Radio listens for 3 hours either side of HW on VHF Ch 16, and works Chs 10 and 11.

*Barry Old Harbour.* The old harbour lies one mile west of Barry Island in Watch House Bay bounded by Knap Point to the west. The harbour, which has a breakwater to the east (2 FG vert), is silted up and dries right out to firm sand. Above half tide, it would afford protection from anything other than southerly; hold to port on entry and then be prepared for shelving sand.

*Barry Old Harbour.* Looking SE at low water. Entrance is in the shallow channel to port on entry. *Water-Wise*

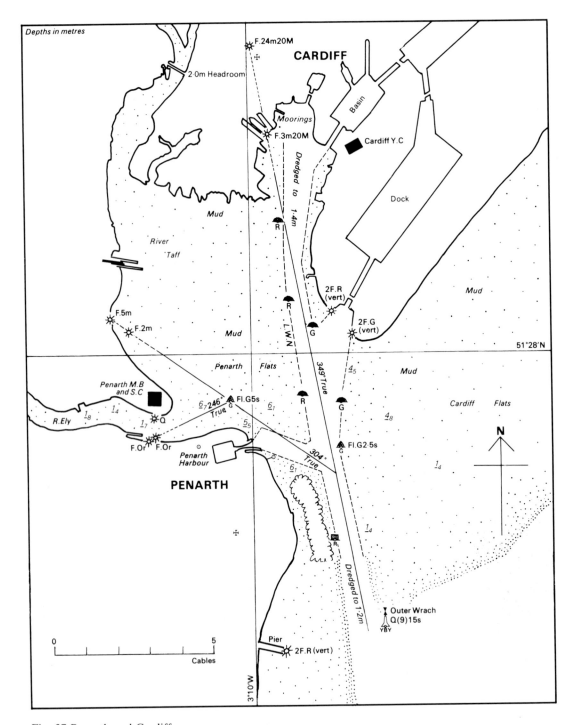

Fig. 37 Penarth and Cardiff.

184

**Penarth**

Rounding Lavernock Point eastbound technically puts the vessel out of the Upper Bristol Channel and into the Severn Estuary (also into the Port of Cardiff's jurisdiction). The entrance is well marked, and craft must keep to the dredged channel (there are rocks off Penarth Head, clear of the channel to port), leaving Outer Wrach (west cardinal) to starboard. The River Ely has 7m (23 ft) depth at HW springs, but dries to a trickle at LW; at LW neaps there are approximately 2m (6 ft 6 ins) near the Penarth Motor Boat and Sailing Club (on the starboard hand entering the river). The River Ely and the approaches to Cardiff generally, dry out to thick mud at low water, but there is reasonable water in the river Ely and main channels at half tide; Penarth harbour dries to soft mud and is usually crowded. The tidal range is up to 11m (36 ft) springs and 6m (20 ft) neaps. Penarth harbour is quite a way from the shops.

**Cardiff**

Pleasure craft will find facilities at the north end of the harbour near the Roath basin (past the Queen's Dock, which is first on the starboard hand going north from Penarth). Cardiff Yacht Club has piped water and electricity on the beach in front of the clubhouse, and visitors should make their needs known to the Club Harbour Master. There is water at the Club slipway for shallow draught vessels for three hours either side of high water, but all moorings dry out.

*Cardiff*. Looking NNE at low water. *Water-Wise*

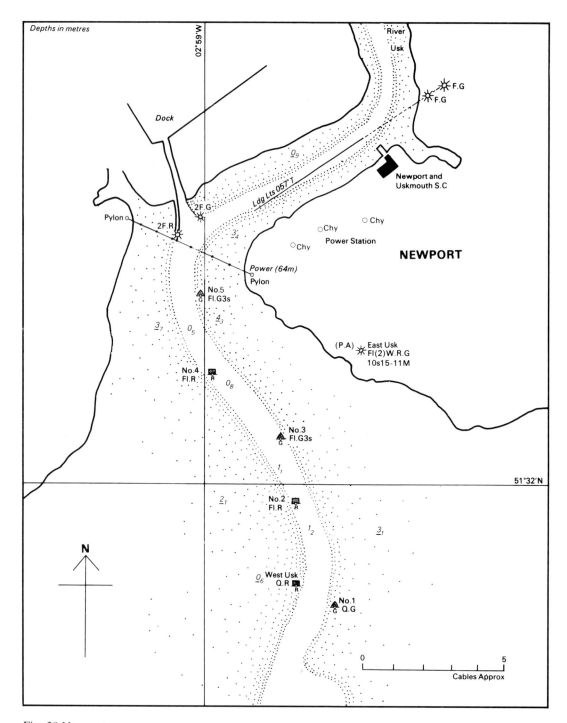

Fig. 38 Newport.

## Newport

The entrance is well buoyed (lateral buoyage). Anchorage in the River Usk affords good holding ground, though ground tackle must be good, because the ebb runs at 4–5 knots at springs (range of tide up to 12m (40 ft) at springs and 6m (20 ft) at neaps). Moorings off the clubhouse (on the starboard hand just past the power station with its tall chimneys) dry out. There are no berths for small craft in the Docks. If leaving to go westward, sail soon after 2 hours before HW to take the ebb. Newport Docks Radio listens on VHF Ch 16 and works Chs 9 and 11, when the tide serves.

## Severn Estuary

If leaving Newport bound east, it is important to take advantage of the full period of flood tide. There are numerous mudbanks which dry to a height of as much as 10m (33 ft), and these should be negotiated with great care if they are covered. Normally the stranger will proceed south to the English and Welsh Grounds Light Float and make for the Bristol Deep. This is well marked with cardinal and lateral buoys (direction of buoyage is up channel towards Bristol).

The tide is fierce in Bristol Deep, and follows the buoyed channel from low water until half tide (when the Welsh Grounds are covered); it then sets NE up the Severn Estuary. Depending on draft, entry to the River Avon may be made after 2½ hours before HW; if necessary to wait, anchor in Portishead Pool, 2½ cables (450m) NE of Portishead Pier; beware that the bay dries out nearly to this line. Anchoring outside Firefly, Outer and Middle buoys is prohibited.

**Charts**

| No | Title | Scale 1: |
|----|-------|----------|
| 1149 | Pendeen to Trevose Head. | 75,000 |
| 1152 | Watchet to Weston super Mare and Barry to Newport. | 50,000 |
| 1156 | Trevose Head to Hartland Point. | 75,000 |
| 1160 | Plans on the coast of Somerset and Devon: | — |
| | Ilfracombe. | 12,500 |
| | Lynmouth; Porlock; Minehead; Watchet. | 20,000 |
| | Barnstaple and Bideford. | 25,000 |
| 1164 | Hartland Point to Ilfracombe, including Lundy. | 75,000 |
| 1165 | Worms Head to Watchet. | 75,000 |
| 1168 | Harbours on the north coast of Cornwall: | — |
| | Newquay bay. | 12,500 |
| | Approaches to Padstow; St Ives bay. | 25,000 |
| 1176 | Severn Estuary – Steep Holen to Avonmouth. | 40,000 |
| | Newport. | 20,000 |
| | Redcliff Bay. | 25,000 |
| 1179 | Bristol Channel. | 150,000 |
| 1159 | Port of Bristol: | — |
| | King Road; River Avon; City docks. | 10,000 |
| Book | *Bristol Channel Yachting Conference Handbook* (See bibliography) | |
| Booklet | *Information for Owners of Pleasurecraft* (See bibliography) | |

**St Ives**

Approaching from the east, leave The Stones off Navax Point, 4 miles short of destination, to port (north cardinal Q); there are drying rocks and a tide race from here SE to Godrevy Island (Fl WR 10s 37m 17/13M), whose red sector shows NW to cover The Stones themselves. Then make 215°T for St Ives Head, keeping Knills Monument (about a mile inland, 166m conspic) open to the east of Tregenna Castle hotel above the shoreline. From the west, clear St Ives Head with its Coastguard Flagstaff until a starboard lateral buoy can be left to starboard (keep 300m (330 yds) offshore to clear off-lying rocks); this buoy marks the submerged end of an old breakwater. St Ives Harbour listens out on VHF Ch 16, and works Chs 14 and 12.

The harbour itself lies between two breakwaters (2 FG vert to starboard, and 2 FR vert to port), and dries out to hard sand; there are many mooring chains on the

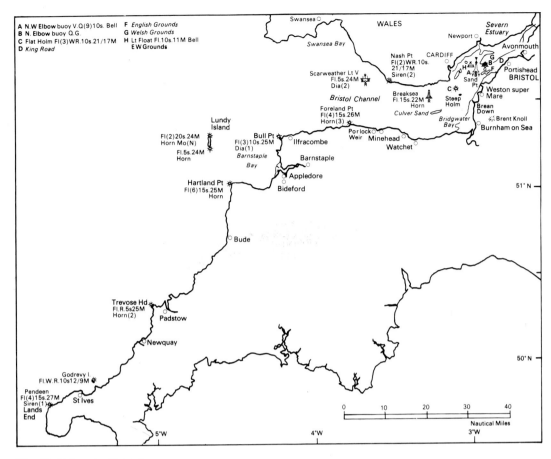

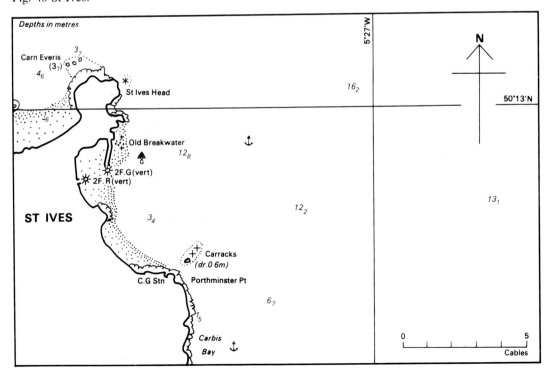

*St Ives.* Looking north at low water. Note the old breakwater stretching eastwards just north of the harbour entrance. *Water-Wise*

bottom. Entry at half tide; range of tide up to 6 metres (20 ft) at springs and up to 2½ metres (8 ft) at neaps. The fetch across the bay produces a heavy swell in onshore winds; a red flag is flown from the south breakwater when it is advisable for pleasure craft to remain in harbour. Shops are plentiful and handy.

The best anchorage is in Carbis Bay one mile to the south, avoiding the Carracks just south of the harbour. Good ground tackle is necessary due to the surge all through St Ives Bay in any onshore wind, but holding is firm throughout the bay.

### Newquay

Newquay harbour lies between two stout stone breakwaters (2 FG to stbd and 2 FR to port) and is well protected; there is a large stone 'island' inside the harbour, which is used by fishing boats. Harbour Master is on duty from Easter to October, and listens out on VHF Ch 16 (working channels 12, 14 and 67).

The bottom dries to hard sand, and is encumbered by mooring chains. Enter above half tide, and be prepared to dry out alongside (if the Harbourmaster can find room). Shops and entertainment are plentiful and handy.

190

*Newquay.* Looking SSE at low water. The stone island inside the harbour is used by fishermen.
*Water-Wise*

Fig. 41 Newquay.

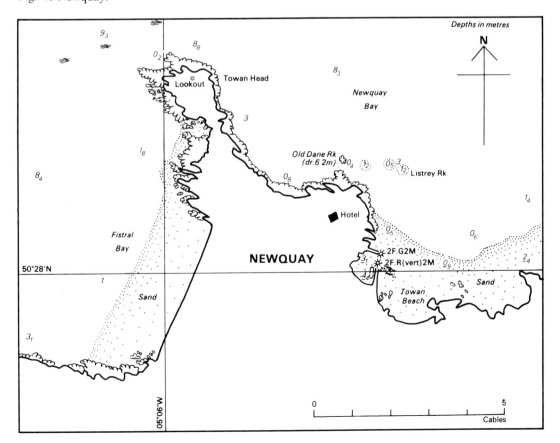

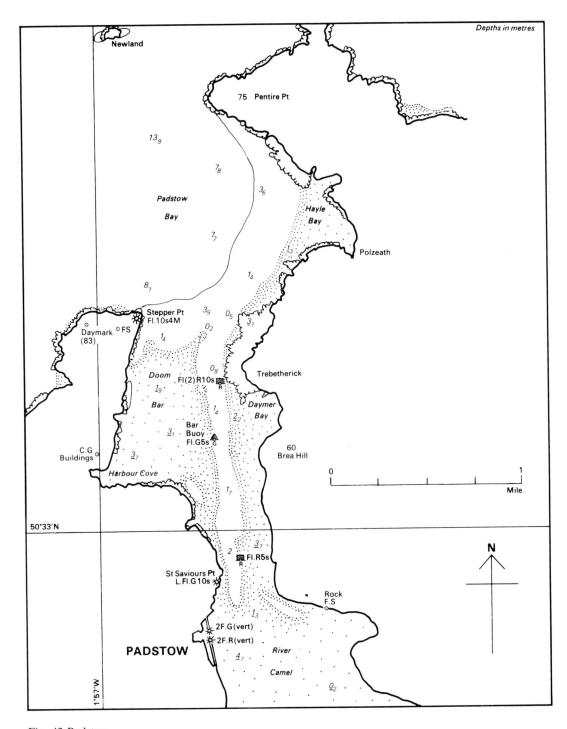

Fig. 42 Padstow.

*Padstow*. Yachts should go into the inner harbour and dry out. *Water-Wise*

### Padstow

Tidal streams off Padstow are generally light by Bristol Channel standards. Entry to Padstow Bay from the north leaves Newland Island and its off-lying dangers to port; from the south, passage may lie inside Gulland Rock, but Gurley Rock and Chimney Rock should be left to starboard. 'Padstow Harbour' listens out on Ch 16 for 12 hours a day in the summer months.

Padstow inner harbour dries out to soft mud which is dredged from time to time (tidal range up to 5½ metres (18 ft) springs and 4 metres (13 ft) neaps), and vessels should wait for half flood before attempting to enter. There is good anchorage east of Stepper Point (Fl 10s 12m 4M), due south of Pentire Point; this positions the boat in the channel, ready to proceed up the river which is buoyed, past Bar Buoy (starboard lateral Fl G 5s) and Brae Buoy (port lateral Fl 2R 10s) to Channel Buoy (port lateral Fl R 5s); there is a Long Flashing Green (10s) light on St Saviour's Point just short of the harbour. The two arms of Padstow harbour each have twin vertical lights, red to port and green to starboard. Enquire for berthing from the Harbour Master; shallow draught keelboats may wait afloat in the pool just down river of the harbour entrance. All moorings are commercially owned, but the port is keen to welcome visitors, and arrangements can usually be made.

### Lundy Island

Tides and overfalls are fierce all round Lundy Island, so it is best to arrive in daylight at slack water and in calm weather. Tide races exist on the flood about one mile to the north and about 1½ miles to the SE of the island, and there are heavy overfalls to the SW and W on the ebb.

193

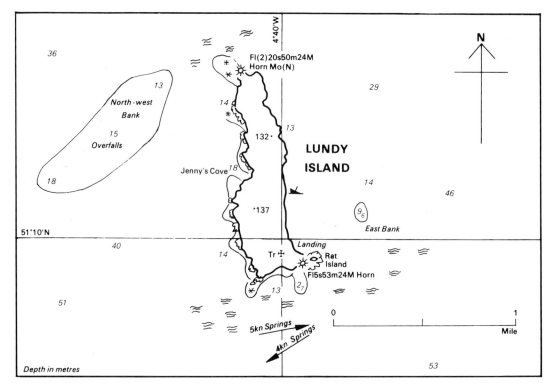

Fig. 43 Lundy Island.

If the wind is from the west, anchor as close as draught permits at the *Landing* indicated at the SE corner of the island on Admiralty chart No 1164; this is in the cove just to the north of the white lighthouse (Fl 5s 53m 24M) which stands 50 feet above the summit of the high ground. There is a stout wire running into the sea which is used by supply boats, and a steep path to the top of the hill. Up to 50m (28 fathoms) of anchor rode will be required at HW.

In easterly winds, use Jenny's Cove on the west coast, but beware of a scend after prolonged westerlies. Tidal range up to 7 metres (23 ft) springs and 3 metres (10 ft) neaps.

**Appledore**

From the north, Morte Stone lies ½ mile off Morte Point and is buoyed (lateral green); the tidal stream makes about 3 knots at springs round the point, but slackens as progress is made south into Barnstaple Bay. The visitor should pass close to Baggy Leap buoy (lateral green) and make for the red and white Bideford Fairway buoy (Safe water mark, L Fl 10s).

From the south, pass 5 miles off Hartland Point (Fl (6) 15s 37m 26M) to avoid the

194

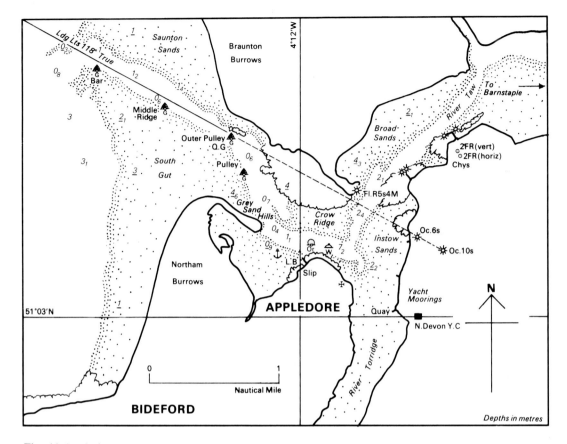

Fig. 44 Appledore.

race and shape directly for Bideford Fairway buoy (L Fl 10s). The southern end of Bideford Bay affords shelter from the south and east, with only weak tidal streams.

Bideford itself may be entered at half tide on the flood; steep seas can develop at the entry at any time, being worst in northerly winds on the ebb. From Bideford Fairway buoy (RW L Fl 10s), the track is 118°T on leading lights Oc 10s (rear) and Oc 6s (front). At Outer Pulley buoy (starboard lateral QG), turn starboard 40 degrees and steer for Inner Pulley buoy (starboard lateral), where the channel is very narrow, and thence close to the spit of land running out from Grey Sands Point, before turning more eastward towards Skerne Point (lifeboat mooring) behind which lies Appledore; the tidal stream can reach 5 knots here at springs. Keelboats should anchor in this area to remain afloat; holding ground is better at the eastern end of the pool. There are good boatyard facilities.

If proceeding up the River Torridge towards Bideford, in general keep over to starboard, and go up after half flood; the bed is constantly changing, so an echo-sounder and local advice is important, as it is to reach Barnstaple. Tidal range

195

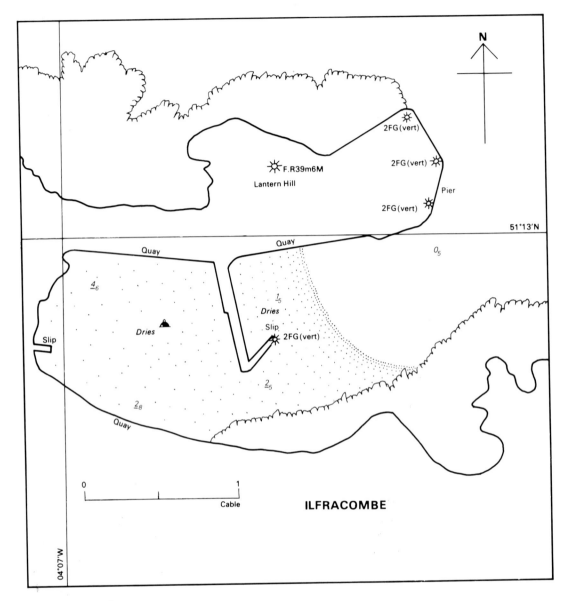

Fig. 45 Ilfracombe.

can be up to 7½ metres (25 ft) springs and 4 metres (13 ft) neaps. Two conspicuous power station chimneys, one hundred feet tall, on the eastern shore north of Instow, are lit by 2 FR vert (north chimney) and 2 FR horiz lights (south chimney).

### Ilfracombe
Ilfracombe offers good protection from the elements. Approaching from the east, leave Copperas Rock to port 4 miles short of destination. From the west, keep at

least ½ mile off Morte Point and Bull Point. If arriving on the ebb, hold close under Lantern Hill (FR 6M) on the northern arm of the harbour to catch a favourable eddy.

The outer bay may be entered by small craft at all states of the tide, but keep towards the quay on the starboard hand to avoid rocks on the southern shore. The harbour dries out, but may be entered at half tide. In the season the port is crowded with commercial and pleasure traffic, so contact the Harbour Master for a berth.

Departing westwards from Ilfracombe, to make for Hartland Point, aim to reach the point, with its race, one hour before LW, i.e. leave Ilfracombe with the last of the flood against you and then carry 5 hours of ebb to Hartland. To avoid the race, stand 5 miles off shore.

Departing eastwards from Ilfracombe, move into the outer harbour when afloat, and then leave 5 hours after HW Swansea, by which time the west-going stream will have lost most of its power, before it turns to the east at or just after LW Swansea.

### Watchet, Minehead and Porlock Weir

These small havens dry right out (tidal range up to 10 metres (33 ft) ), and may only be entered above half tide, even by vessels only drawing one metre. There are hazards lying offshore at all three, so that local knowledge or a close study of Chart No 1160 (or the *Bristol Yachting Conference Handbook*) is essential, even for entry in good weather by day. Strangers wishing to wait for a tide, or to shelter from weather anywhere from the south, should anchor in Blue Anchor Road; good ground tackle is essential, because the tidal stream runs at up to 5 knots.

### Burnham on Sea

Bridgwater Bay is a mass of shoals, and the tidal range is up to 11 metres (37 ft) springs and 6 metres (20 ft) neaps. In brisk conditions the waters are confused and broken; stranding can be hazardous. In calm weather craft drawing up to 1¾ metres can enter across the flats, but should follow the channel where possible, taking frequent soundings; buoyage may be unreliable after strong winds due to shifting sands changing the channel.

Find Bridgwater Bar buoy (Fl R 2.5s), when Flatholm Island will be just closing Steepholm Island from the east, and steer east for Brent Knoll. This is the tallest feature (133m – 435 ft) on a flat landscape behind the town, and the channel will normally lie between lateral buoys with the white sector of Burnham Light (F WRG 077°–079°T and Fl 7.5s 28m 17M conspic) showing Brent Knoll just open to the south.

No 4 buoy (QR) marks the cut through Gore Sands to the north, passable 2 hours before HW by keeping Flatholm lighthouse just open to the east of Steepholm Island astern, to make good a track of 165°T (beware strong tidal stream on the flood).

Nos 5 and 7 starboard hand buoys (No 7 is lit: Fl G 5s) bring the entrance track round to starboard, until new leading marks are in line on 102°T (white vertical

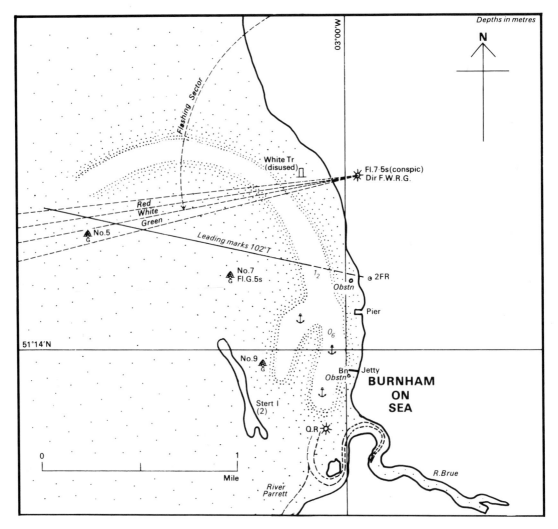

Fig. 46 Burnham on Sea. With Stert Island.

mark on sea wall, and church tower; both FR). When 250 metres offshore (beware stone obstruction – paddling pool – 100m offshore at this point), steer south for the stone jetty and beacon. Bilge keelers may take the ground east of Stert Island or by Stert Point; keelboats can sit upright in soft mud in the River Brue (enquire at yacht club on north bank of the river, near the entrance). Most of the shops are just inland from the front.

Leaving Burnham to go westwards, keep Brent Knoll just open to the south of the conspicuous entry light ½ mile north of the church (Fl 7.5s 28m 17M and F WRG 24m 16, 12, 12M). This gives 258° in the white sector of the fixed light and is just on

*Burnham on Sea.* The white mark on the sea wall and the church tower leading marks are both lit, for those bold enough to try the entry at night. *Water-Wise*

the southern end of the arc of the flashing light's arc of visibility, and leads between lateral marks numbered from 5 down to 1 (after No 7, only the port red marks No 4 and No 2 – leave to starboard on departing – are lit). On passing between Nos 1 and 2 buoys shape course to lie due west and pass close aboard the red and white Gore Buoy (safe water mark, Iso 5s) until Minehead is sighted 22 miles further on.

### Weston-super-Mare

The passage between Bristol and Weston-super-Mare may be direct if above half tide, but there are extensive drying sands on the English Grounds which make a detour necessary via the English and Welsh Grounds Light Float at other times. The tidal stream exceeds 5 knots at springs, and planning should take this into account.

199

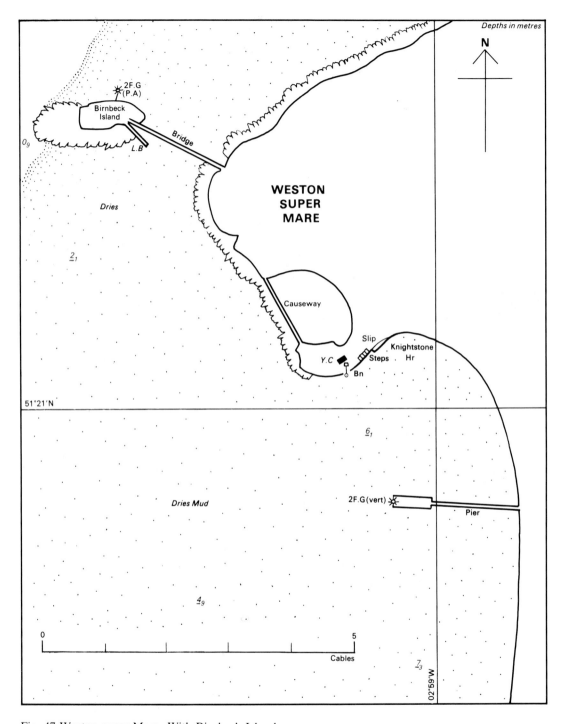

Fig. 47 Weston super Mare. With Birnbeck Island.

*Weston super Mare.* Knightstone harbour is really only an open stretch of drying sand, with a wall along the north-east side. The Weston Bay YC is just off the picture to the left. *Water-Wise*

As a matter of technical interest, the vessel passes out of the Severn Estuary at Sand Point. When sailing north-east to Weston, the various sands and islands (notably Culver Sand and Steepholm Is) are buoyed. The conspicuous feature of Brean Down will be discernible as the southern end of Weston Bay is approached, and the navigator may notice gliders flying from the grass airfield just south of Weston-super-Mare.

In Weston Bay itself, there is always a southerly set, which fluctuates with the state of the tide; the whole bay between Birnbeck Island and Brean Down dries out to mud. The range of tide is up to 11 metres (37 ft) at springs and 6½ metres (22 ft) at neaps.

Knightstone harbour (7 knots speed limit) dries to a hard flat bottom inshore, and there are some mooring chains. It can be entered two hours either side of HW; legs are necessary for keelboats. There is a beacon on the northern shore, just to seaward of a slipway and steps (no mooring alongside); the pier to the south has 2 FG (vert) lights, and should not be approached too closely due to the southerly set. Weston Bay Yacht Club just above the harbour works VHF Ch 'M' at summer weekends during the evenings. The shops are handy to the harbour.

If leaving Weston to proceed further up the Bristol Channel, the vessel technically

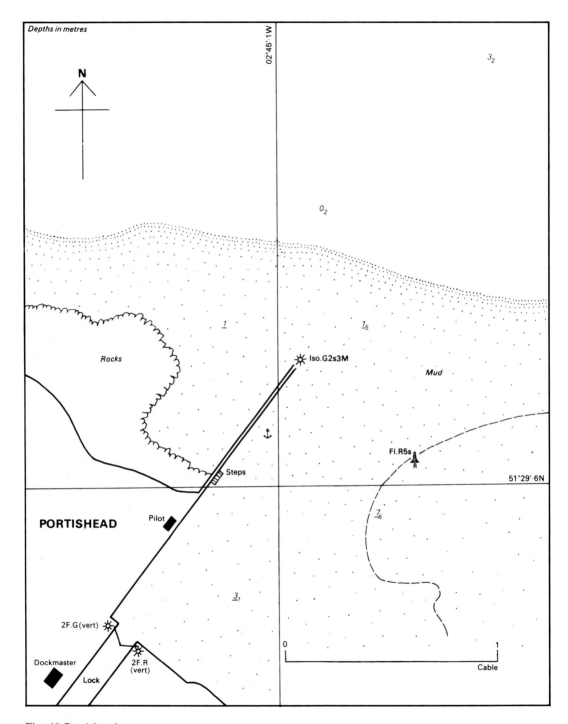

Fig. 48 Portishead.

202

enters the Severn Estuary at Sand Point (but there is no line on the water, and no noticeable effect on the helm). The English Grounds have extensive areas of drying sand, so that the state of tide (and depth of keel) may require a passage via NW Elbow west cardinal buoy (VQ (9) 10s), and N Elbow green lateral buoy (QG).

### Portishead

For economic reasons the port is closed except in an emergency. Entry lies between the pierhead (Iso G 2s 3M) and red lateral buoy (Fl R 5s); on the flood, there is an eddy which sets towards the pier (the tide turns westward 3½ hours before HW). Firefly rocks lie 350m (400 yds) NNW of the pierhead, and have a least depth of less than a metre (starboard lateral Fl (2) G 5s). Boats awaiting the lock gates should contact the Dockmaster for instructions or, if he is not available, contact Avonmouth Radio on VHF Ch 16; the channel dries to soft mud two hours either side of LW. Anchoring overnight should only be done by prior arrangement, and is available in 3m (10 ft) of water 4 cables (730m) NE of the lock gates (in Portishead Pool) sheltered from southwesterly winds; a tripping line is advised.

### Avonmouth

Skippers of small craft approaching Avonmouth should exercise great vigilance and give a wide berth to commercial vessels manoevring in the area; see below for *Radio*. Off the entrance to the Avon, the tidal stream runs up to 5 knots at springs (being stronger on the flood) and up to 3 knots at neaps, apart from 30 mins either side of HW. Entry leaves the commercial dock with its three piers to port, and the visitor should hold close to the south pier (Oc RG 30s 10M, first in the green sector then in the red); leading marks FR on 127°T (by day, white post in line with mast) – there is shallow water south and west of the leading line. The other piers up the Severn have further lights which should be identified at night. When the second set of leading marks to starboard (white posts Oc 5s) are in line on 173°T, turn to this heading and from then on keep to the middle of the channel. There is a speed limit of 6 knots in the river for vessels drawing more than 1.9m (6 ft 3 ins); shallower draft vessels are limited to 9 knots.

Due to the fast tidal stream, very good ground tackle is needed in the lower reaches of the River Avon, but anchoring is not encouraged due to the movements of commercial traffic. Boats which can take soft mud are advised to moor alongside the Portishead Cruising Club iron jetty at Pill; keel boats must lie into the jetty. Prior arrangement is both courteous and necessary, as the club is not open continuously (PCC, The Clubhouse, Pump Square, Pill, Bristol).

### Bristol

The Floating Harbour at Bristol is protected by the Cumberland Basin, with Entrance Lock at its western end and Junction Lock at its eastern end; both these are on the northern side of Cumberland Basin, and both have swing bridges which

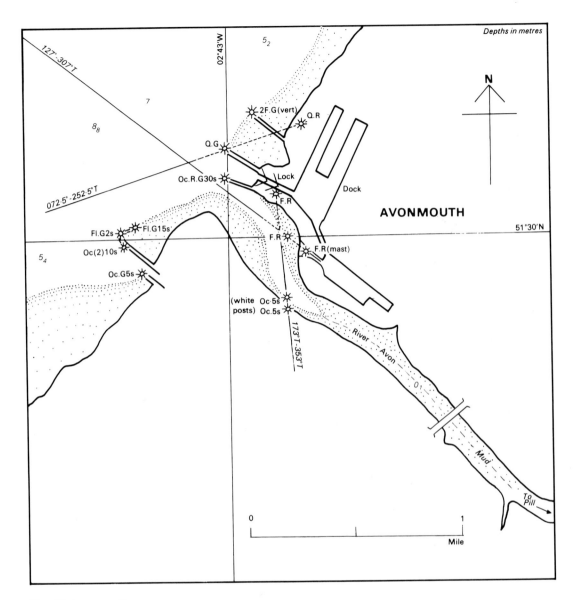

Fig. 49 Avonmouth.

are subject to priority road traffic during rush hours (they do not open 0800–0900 and 1700–1800 hrs), and to state of tide; arrival by HW is recommended. The visitor is recommended to obtain the Bristol City Docks booklet (*Information for Owners of Pleasurecraft*, Harbour Master, City Docks, Underfall Yard, Cumberland Road, Bristol), and to get instructions by radio; boats without radio must hoist or sound 'R' when passing the signal station at Avonmouth and proceed according to the information booklet. The dockmaster's office is on the south quay by the Entrance

*Avonmouth.* Looking SE from the mouth at half-tide. *Water-Wise*

Lock, and vessels arriving for entry should wait at Hotwells Pontoon for the green signal before approaching the lock entrance. If instructions are required, tie up at Tongue Head (knuckle just upstream of the entrance) and report to the Dockmaster. When in the lock, stay near the entrance to avoid turbulence while it is being filled. Steady small craft by hand on one of the fixed ladders; larger vessels will need 25 metres of line fore and aft slipped round bollards ashore, unless a large commercial ship allows tying alongside. If a vessel misses the last lock, a gridiron is available on which she may safely dry out – permission for use from the Dockmaster; alternatively she should lie on the centre line of the lock gates, 25m out.

*Radio*
Use low power to call on VHF Ch 16 and be prepared to switch to Ch 12 or 14. Call 'Avonmouth Radio' approaching King Road (off Portishead), and 'City Docks Radio' when upstream of Black Rock light, i.e. before entering the Avon Gorge.

*Caution*
There are overhead bridges, locks with specific times of opening related to water level and road traffic, a swift current, traffic priorities, semaphore and light signals, and local bye laws. These are too numerous to mention in detail here, and the visitor should obtain the Bristol City Docks information booklet referred to above.

*Facilities*
The booklet similarly details the various facilities available, from repairs to sewage disposal, from fresh water to visitors' moorings. In connection with the last named, visitors should contact the River and Canal Foreman as soon as possible (only after arrival) to obtain a mooring allocation. Bathing is not recommended without tetanus, paratyphoid and typhoid inoculations.

**Bibliography**

*Bristol Channel Yachting Conference Handbook*
*Cruising Guide to Anglesey and the Menai Strait* Robert Kemp
*Cruising Guide to the Isle of Man* Robert Kemp
*Information for Owners of Pleasurecraft* Bristol Harbour Master
*Harbours in and Around Morecambe Bay* Blackpool and Fleetwood YC, Skippool Creek.
*Solway Firth Sailing Directions and Anchorages* Solway SC, Kippford.
*The Clyde Cruising Club Pilot*
*The Irish Cruising Club Pilot*

Other sources
*Admiralty Pilot*
*Chart Catalogue – Home Edition*
*MacMillans's and Reed's Nautical Almanacs*
*Ravenglass Boatowners Association*
*Solva Boatowners Association*

# Index